COUPLE THERAPY AND INFIDELITY RECOVERY

The Workbook On Communication Skills To Overcome Jealousy, Anxiety And Betrayal In a Relationship. The Best Help To Rescue The Marriage After An Affair

LEIL MILLER - ALEATHA CLOUD

TABLES OF CONTENTS:

- INTRODUCTION 3
- PART 1: SECTION I – COUPLES THERAPY 6
- WHY COUPLES GO TO COUPLES THERAPY 7
- WHY CONSIDER COUPLE'S THERAPY? 15
- SECTION II – TYPES OF RELATIONSHIP AND SOLUTIONS 22
- ANXIETY AND JEALOUSY IN RELATIONSHIP 23
- INSECURE IN LOVE 31
- DOMINATE YOURSELF IN LOVE TO OVERCOME THE FEAR OF ABANDONMENT AND CODEPENDENT RELATIONSHIP 38
- TOXIC RELATIONSHIP 43
- NARCISSISTIC RELATIONSHIP 48
- UNDERSTANDING HOW NOT TO ATTRACT PEOPLE WITH PERSONALITY DISORDER 55
- SECTION III: COUPLES COMMUNICATION 60
- COUPLES COMMUNICATION 61
- RELATIONSHIP QUESTIONS FOR COUPLES 69
- BEST RELATIONSHIP ACTIVITIES FOR COUPLES 74
- COUPLES COUNSELING EXERCISES, WORKSHEETS, & TECHNIQUES ... 78
- EXERCISES FOR COUPLES 87
- IMPROVE INTIMACY WITH YOUR PARTNER 100
- MAINTAINING YOUR RELATIONSHIP 106
- PART 2: SECTION I – UNDERSTANDING INFIDELITY 114
- INTRODUCTION 115
- WHAT IS INFIDELITY? 118
- HEAL FROM INFIDELITY 126
- MEN AND WOMEN: DIFFERENCES 132
- SECTION II – HEALING FROM INFIDELITY 137
- THE FIRST PHASE: THE CRISIS PHASE 138
- THE SECOND PHASE: THE ROLE OF GRIEF 142
- THE THIRD PHASE: UNDERSTANDING 148
- ACCEPTANCE – LOVE YOURSELF 156
- THE FOURTH PHASE: MAKING A WISE DECISION 163
- MAKE YOUR CHOICE 170
- THE FIFTH PHASE: RECONNECTION 176
- EMBRACING SELF - FORGIVENESS 182
- REBOOTING YOUR RELATIONSHIP 189
- THE SIXTH PHASE: LOVE AND START AGAIN 196
- EXERCISES TO RECONNECT WITH YOUR PARTNER 204
- THE 7-STEP RECOVERY MAP 208
- SEX AS A COUPLE 211
- CONCLUSION 218

Introduction

Most couples simply don't know how to reach solutions together because they were never given the correct tools. Look at this as a toolbox to help you with any issues you may run into in your relationship.

Even though married couples often don't know how to resolve their issues when left to their own devices, they find that it isn't nearly as hard as they thought when they have something to work with. This is exactly what provides you with: something to work with.

Without it, your conversation with your spouse will go in every direction it can. As you may already know from your personal experience, this kind of conversation doesn't land either of you in a place you want to be.

It might be difficult sometimes, but there is no other option than to use the questions given to you here to help sort through the problems in your marriage. They get to the heart of every issue in marriage. That's because all of them are concerned foremost with issues in your communication, from which all problems ultimately stem.

I hope you can come to see them through all of these questions. That theme is to deal with one problem at a time. It is natural for couples to bicker with each other, each feeling justified for defending their side of the story. Everyone thinks they are right.

But no one "wins" if not even a single individual issue is addressed. When you and your spouse keep bickering, even if you are absolutely certain you are right — it doesn't matter that you are right. You won't get anywhere talking to them in this way. It simply isn't productive communication.

Productive communication is the final goal of this, and of dialectical behavior therapy in general. It means really understanding what your partner is saying, even if you still don't agree. You have to hear what they are saying if you want them to listen to you. When both spouses do nothing more than arguing without end, no one accomplishes anything.

By tackling these questions one at a time, you will reach a full understanding of what your spouse believes — not just a caricature of it.

The best strategy is to describe your relationship and compare it to discover where your visions of yourselves as a couple differ. There are sure to be discrepancies between how your partner sees your relationship and how you see it.

Tackle these questions head-on. At some point, you need to come to an agreement on who you are as a couple. You are just going to keep fighting even more if you don't even have the same image of your relationship. This image informs your aspirations and hopes for the future, so it matters deeply.

Once you at least come to a greater agreement on your self-identity as a couple, I want you to take a moment to address all the times you haven't lived up to this image.

See their views as they are: coming from a personal place as yours do for you. It will help you get into their mind and understand them.

Give yourselves some space to think about this question on your own. This part of the exercise is important because sometimes we have the truth as we share it with others, but then there is a different truth that we feel when we are alone.

When you have the space to be open with yourself, consider how you really see your relationship. Who do you see yourselves as, even if you wouldn't ever tell your spouse this? Ultimately, you will need to share it with your spouse.

It isn't healthy for your relationship to keep things from each other. You need to feel like you can't be honest about what you think. If you don't feel comfortable sharing with your partner how you feel about your relationship, then you have already found one major cause of issues that needs to be addressed. You may have many other issues to work through, but this is one that absolutely must be confronted.

At the end of the day, couples who do not trust each other enough to speak their mind cannot be healthy and conscious. You should be able to be open about how you view yourselves as a couple. If you can't, this is the first issue you need to tackle. Read on in the workbook to learn how you should tackle it. Please enjoy!

PART 1: Section I – Couples Therapy

Why Couples go to Couples Therapy

Simple couple therapy is designed to access therapy that is accessible and does not require careful thought or understanding (something that most people find too difficult to use and apply) to be useful. On the other hand, they are not coupling stupid enough to deny them when they need help or too guilty to fight them when they give them. Nor is it for newly trained therapists who feel they need to listen and indulge in unnecessary and unnecessary fear of not disturbing their clients.

After years of seeing couples blaming themselves and blaming themselves or being victimized without any responsibility for any of their problems and after being exhausted, they came in to prevent them from acting on self-destruction or some destructive impulses, and couple therapy has become much more straightforward and more transparent. However, not all are.

It is not for couples where, instead of trying to strengthen and improve their relationship, each couple must be right and find their way. It is natural for people to want to be correct and to find their way and to be disappointed when they do not. It is even natural that some people are right and find a way to get angry when they don't have it.

Each of them can be tolerated, spoken and even overcome. However, whenever either partner has to be right and find their way, anything threatening or wrong, or if they can't find their way, will be seen as an attack and will do everything possible to defend his position resisted and retaliated.

Instead, it involves teaching and teaching each partner how to manage and resolve emerging conflicts fully. As a result, most people avoid conflict not because they do not have the will to fix it, but because they do not have the means to do so. Also, they feel that managing conflict will only get worse and have little confidence that it will improve.

As partners acquire the skills to effectively manage disagreements, disappointments, troubles and make things better without getting worse, each develops emotional tenacity, self-esteem, and self-esteem. Add practical conflict resolution skills and tools that come from mindfulness and positive psychology, and any motivated couple can embark on a shared future that compensates for the emotional baggage they still have of their genes (nature) and foster (feed).

What Factors Affect the Couple's Relationship?

Many factors can affect the relationship and cause problems in the relationship. The elements can come from an internal or external partner.

Internal factors affecting the couple relationship:

- Alcohol and drug abuse, sexual dissatisfaction sickness etc.

External factors affecting the couple relationship:

- Frequent job changes the problem in the office a problem in the community etc.

How to know when the Time is Right for Couples Therapy

If you have problems and can't solve them, you need a therapist. When you need a therapist, a sign appears, such as:

I cannot sleep concentration problems feelings of dissatisfaction in marriage emotional stress, drastic weight fluctuations etc.

How to find a therapist for couples?

There are many therapeutic resources on the Internet, in the yellow pages, and magazines. It's like looking for a lawyer, an insurance agency, or a doctor. Some information may not be right, so you should tell your family, social service agencies, community information centers, or couple therapy associations.

How long is the couple therapy?

It depends on the problems, the effort and time you are willing to devote to your healing and growth, and the focus of the therapist. Some need 5 to 12 sessions in a few months.

Each session lasts approximately 75 minutes to 100 minutes. The therapist usually gives the estimated time when designing a treatment plan. Discuss it during the first sessions.

Should the couple make an appointment together or separately?

He recommends that the husband and wife meet for the first time. After the first session, the therapist can recommend meeting a person or a couple.

A particular person has saved many relationships. The procedure is usually initiated by one person who wants to keep the relationship, while the other person does not want to force it. Over time, an unprepared person sees the changes in a specific person and the positive impact they have on the relationship. Then they start to come in and get more involved in the renewal process.

The simple truth about relationships is that you can't get anyone to do anything, and even if you try it won't work, but what you can do is change the way you communicate with your partner. When you do this, over time, you will start to change the other person's behavior without trying to force them to change. It is the only way to create lasting change, and change must come from within and cannot be forced.

Even if both partners are ready to work on your relationship, the real change comes from within. In other words, the first thing you should improve your relationship with is to work on yourself. Most of the time, you know where your short term arrivals are, if you have communication problems, privacy issues or whatever, and working on yourself is the best place to start repairing your relationship.

The truth is that it is difficult to know what to expect. Every specialist will have an alternate degree of experience and different methods of solving their problems. It is, therefore, essential to find a therapist with whom you feel comfortable. You should be able to talk about your issues without feeling judgment or therapy.

So to find a good one, answer and call, ask a lot of questions and try to find the one you're comfortable talking to. Make sure they are ready to create a viable plan of action with you, as the real goal of therapy should be to provide you with the tools you need to deal with any non-therapeutic situation.

If you decide to go this route, here are some things to know. First of all, therapy can get expensive quickly, and it is doubtful that you will be able to solve your problems in one session, so make sure you are ready to deploy some mass. Second, you may learn things about your partner that can completely ruin your relationship. Sometimes therapy brings stuff you wish you never learned, so stay tuned.

Excellent communication is the key to a happy relationship among others. Divorce rates in the United States and around the world are not practical. Couple therapy aims to resolve the problem between husband and wife to lead a happy life without severe conflict or heated discussions. The therapist or psychologist helps the married couple to identify the problem and suggest behaviors and other modifications to satisfy both parties. Couple therapy is a combination of education, mediation and psychotherapy.

The nature of the correspondence between couples is the most vital factor that recognizes upbeat relationships from despondent marriages. The ability to communicate well is also the best indicator of satisfaction and the stability of the relationship over time. As such, the quantity of issues, singular character characteristics or contrasts of supposition has nothing to do with happy or miserable relationships. Instead, couples talk about their problems and their differences. Communication is essential, and it is believed that communication skills can be quickly learned.

Each couple has their problems; and during couple therapy with the help of psychologists, determine the cause of the problem. For instance, if a couple contends a ton, during the meetings, they make them think about the reasons for these arguments and find a solution. Resolution can change the way they interact or react to different situations or changes in behavior.

Being married and having a healthy relationship takes a lot of work. This requires the work of both parties involved in the relationship. When a relationship hits the big rocks, you can seek advice or therapy. Sometimes emotion-focused couple therapy can help you find deeper problems in your emotions. One of the best types of in-frame therapy is emotion-focused couple therapy. Most therapies will only bring the relationship back to what it was before, but the theory behind emotionally targeted therapy programs is to make the relationship even more reliable.

If you are looking for a more Christian or spiritual understanding of therapy, you should try emotionally focused couples. This service practices the application of the New Testament on how to treat and act on one another. Often, we forget what our roles are. The Bible tells us that a husband must "love his wife as Christ loved the church". This means that a husband must love his wife, no matter what she does, no matter how much he has treated her, no matter what! The wife must submit to her husband. This means that the woman must obey her husband; he is the head of the family, respect him. The wife tries to guide her husband too often, which in turn sends a message to her husband that she does not recognize him. This will cause the husband to stop showing that he loves his wife. The vicious circle continues indefinitely until we decide to stop it.

Psychotherapy is a practice used to perform emotionally directed couple therapy. This can be accomplished through conversation, works of art, theatre, music or therapeutic touch. Psychotherapy uses many philosophical approaches during therapy. The term psychotherapy is interchangeable with counseling. Many people prefer to call this advice. Client and patient confidentiality are expected as many personal items will be shared as long as they exist. In today's world, sessions can be conducted face to face, by phone or even online. There is no limit to how long a person heals, or in the case of couples treating other people. It's a different time for each person. Some people complete therapy within a week, while others take years.

Is there a cheaper alternative to couple therapy that can be done at home?

That's a great question, YES, there are fantastic home courses that have a better success rate (for a fraction of the price) than traditional couple therapy. Most of these home courses are focused on the future, not on mentioning the past, which, frankly, is what you want anyway.

They will help you continue your relationship, even if you are the only one who wants to work on it. With most of these home courses, you get a proven path of action that allows you to continually improve your relationship, even if you're about to get divorced. You get detailed instructions to rekindle your relationship with its former glory, also if it's been years that you honestly can't say you're happy.

These home courses start by teaching you how to connect more deeply, which solves all other problems about 1,000 times more easily because nobody wants to solve problems with someone with whom they do not have a stable relationship. Some couples have even found that once they had a healthy relationship, most of their other problems seemed to go away. This is why it is so essential to take this vital first step and reconnect with your partner.

Why Consider Couple's Therapy?

When someone is struggling with their mental health, regardless of whether or not they have a diagnosed condition, therapy can be very helpful. The same goes for relationships, whether there is a major problem or not. A lot of people believe couples counseling is just for people on the verge of a breakdown, but the reality is that just about every couple can benefit. Communication can be very tricky and there are ups and downs in every relationship. A good counselor can facilitate difficult conversations, provide insight into what couples are trying to say, or just help a couple with communication techniques. This describes different scenarios where therapy can help, as well as guidelines on finding the best therapist for you and your partner.

Why Consider Couples Therapy

When should a couple consider therapy? There are lots of scenarios where a relationship can benefit from the advice and guidance of a third party, and they aren't all emotionally catastrophic. Here are seven:

You don't trust each other

Trust is the glue that keeps a relationship together. If it's broken, either through emotional or physical cheating, lying about money, or lies about anything, the relationship stalls and starts to break down. Either one person within the couple or both no longer feel safe and secure. A therapist can help heal the division, facilitate vulnerability, and offer guidance on what to do.

You fight all the time

Some couples argue more than others, but if you realize you are fighting with your partner more than you usually do, it's a sign that something is wrong. It could be about anything small or big. The issue is that most of your communication becomes contentious and stressful. A counselor can help you find out why arguing has become your go-to communication style and what to do about it.

You just don't communicate well

You don't have to be in conflict with your partner to benefit from therapy. Sometimes, you and your partner just don't "get" each other. Communication-wise, it feels like you are ships passing in the night. It's always a struggle to express your thoughts and feelings about things, and you frequently feel misunderstood or even ignored. On the other hand, you might feel disconnected from your partner and unable to get anything out of them, emotionally. Maybe both are present in your relationship. A therapist can help you safely break down walls, be more vulnerable, and learn to communicate more.

You're going through a huge life change

Change is always difficult for a relationship, even if it's a good change. It can throw off your normal routines, emotional state, and even your identity. Changes in relationships can include moving house, getting a new job, losing a job, losing a loved one, having kids, and soon. It can be very hard to express your feelings (and even identify your feelings) to your partner, so therapy can be very beneficial. They can help you and your partner be vulnerable and honest with each other, understand each other more, and strengthen your bond.

Physical intimacy is a point of conflict

Everyone (and every couple) is different when it comes to physical intimacy. It can cause a lot of conflicts, especially if one person in the relationship feels rejected, neglected, or pressured physically. It's a very sensitive and emotional topic, and frustrations can flare. A therapist can help keep things cool and collected, and provide a safe space for vulnerability and honesty.

One (or both) people in the relationship have mental health issues

Mental health issues like depression, anxiety, bipolar, and more have a big effect on a relationship. Navigating a relationship can be especially tricky if only one of the people has the diagnosis, and is having trouble communicating their needs to their partner. Maybe you have social anxiety and wish your partner would be more considerate about triggers, or your partner (who isn't mentally ill) is confused about what to do when you go through a depression episode. A therapist can help you two communicate and understand each other better.

Something just feels "off"

Therapy isn't just for couples who know exactly what they want to talk about. If something just feels "off" or wrong about your relationship, you should strongly consider therapy. A therapist can help you identify areas and triggers where the discomfort is strongest, and express your feelings and fears to your partner in a clear, honest way. It may turn out that you two just needed a third party to help clarify some things, or it may reveal deeper issues that you can focus on.

Couples therapy is not a magic solution to all of your problems as a couple or as an individual. Not every relationship can (or should) be saved, so don't go into couple's therapy expecting to walk out with a perfect, shiny new relationship. Couples therapy should teach you better communication, but communicating better may reveal things that let you know the relationship shouldn't continue. This isn't easy to hear, but it's important to accept that going to couples' therapy may not give you the happy ending you expect.

Couples therapy should also not be treated as something that only happens in the therapist's office. Don't plan on going once a week or once every two weeks, and not doing anything else. That won't actually improve communication between you and your partner. Like regular therapy, most of the work is actually done outside of that hour or so window. The therapist's job is to help identify areas of conflict, give advice on what to do, and facilitate dialogue, but it's up to you and your partner to actually put things into action.

Are there Couples who shouldn't go to Therapy?

Believe it or not, there are certain circumstances where a couple should not go to couples' therapy. If both people in the couple aren't willing to do work on themselves, feel painful emotions, and be vulnerable with their partner, couples' therapy will not work. Instead, the best way to improve the relationship is through individual therapy.

Most couple's therapists also don't recommend therapy for abusive relationships. Abuse doesn't go away through better communication; it's a deeper issue. The abuser will usually not take responsibility for their own actions, and will try to manipulate the therapy to get the end goal they want. This is usually total control over their partner, who blames themselves for the abuse. Couples therapy can actually be dangerous for the abuse, since anything they say in the therapist's office might trigger their partner's anger once they've left. According to The National Domestic Violence Hotline, abuse isn't a "relationship" problem, so it isn't something that couples' therapy will help.

How to Find the right Therapist

For couple's therapy to be effective, you need the right therapist. How do you track one down? Here are some tips:

Make sure the therapist is qualified

The very first step when searching for a couple's therapist is making sure they're educated and have the right qualifications. Look up counselors on websites like the National Registry of Marriage-Friendly Therapists, The Gottman Institute Referral Directory, and the American Association of Marriage and Family Therapists. If you just Google therapists in your area or hear about one through word-of-mouth, make sure they are licensed to practice therapy. Look for licenses like LMFT (licensed marriage and family therapist) and EFT (emotionally-focused couple's therapy).

There's nothing wrong with asking a therapist questions about their qualifications. Some good ones include, "How long have you been practicing couples' therapy?" and "What kind of advanced training do you have?"

Find out their opinion on marriage and divorce

Before committing to a therapist, it's a good idea to find out if they lean one way or the other when it comes to divorce. Some therapists really care about keeping marriages together, while others are neutral. It isn't really ethical to suggest divorce for a couple if they haven't brought it up, but it isn't unheard of. By knowing what the therapist's bias is, you can decide if they are the right fit for your relationship goals or not. You can ask questions like:

- Do you believe all marriages can be saved?
- What's your view on divorce?
- What circumstances would make you believe divorce is the best option for a couple?

Trust your gut

You should feel comfortable with your therapist. You should also feel like they "get" you, even when you have trouble expressing your feelings and thoughts as clearly as you would like. Therapists are trained for a reason; they should be able to listen and - if what you said is confusing - help you clarify it for yourself and your partner. It can take 2-3 sessions to feel comfortable, but if you still aren't at ease, it may be time to try another therapist. Don't worry about offending them. They aren't interested in wasting your time or theirs with a counseling partnership that isn't working. How do you know if the therapist isn't the right fit? Watch out for signs and feelings like:

- They're always siding with your partner and you feel ganged up on.
- They're pressuring you to do something you don't want to do.
- You don't feel like the therapist is on the same page about your relationship goals.
- You don't feel respected or listened to.
- They think there's one "right" way of doing things and having a successful marriage.
- They're using language that makes you feel ashamed of your feelings and judged.

While you're deciding if a therapist is the right one for you, focus on what you're feeling. Don't spend time worrying about what your partner thinks. That being said, you should definitely ask your partner how they feel about the therapist after you've accessed yourself. The goal is to find a therapist that makes both of you feel respected and comfortable.

Section II – Types of Relationship and Solutions

Anxiety and Jealousy in Relationship

Nearly every facet of a relationship is affected by anxiety, no matter what type. When someone enters into a relationship, there are relatively simple expectations that go along with it. First and foremost, you assume the other person can fulfill the role of a partner. Being a partner involves a solid ability to communicate openly, offer companionship, contribute financially, hold onto a stable job, and eventually raise a family.

Relationship Communication

As you should know, communication is particularly important when it comes to romantic relationships. Being able to discuss all issues freely, make plans, and set goals for the future are all vital for a successful relationship. Otherwise, how could two partners handle their responsibilities, challenges, and expectations?

Relationship Communication Anxiety

Anxiety has a severe emotional effect on people, and the partner is always affected in some way as a result of seeing his or her significant other suffering and going through the whole life crippling experience. And many cases in which the one suffering from anxiety will suppress any emotion or feeling. Emotions carry a great deal of power, and some people find it too challenging to face them. Those who are afraid to express themselves emotionally have likely lived in a household where the behavior was discouraged.

Communication anxiety can also oppositely manifest itself without involving any emotion suppression. For instance, let's say your partner unloads only her most powerful feelings and emotions regularly. Some people cannot hold back on certain beliefs, so they lash out, and as a result, both of you end up feeling overwhelmed and confused, leading to another problem. Experiencing these outbursts often enough, you can start feeling that it's your job to find a solution to your partner's issues. It's not enough to notice the anxiety and the strain it's putting on your relationship. You get the feeling you are the sole savior of this partnership. Unfortunately, this usually makes things worse as your partner could start developing resentment towards you for their behavior.

Another communication problem is when you consider expressing yourself as a risky affair. Maybe you are wondering what will happen if you reveal what you honestly think. It is enough to trigger your anxiety as you are afraid of the uncertainty of the outcome. Frequently, this symptom stems from not having confidence in yourself and you are worried about an adverse reaction from your partner. In this case, you might be taking a great deal of time to rehearse what you will say and complicate things further by imagining all the possible scenarios.

Social Situations

Being in certain social situations is difficult for many people who don't even suffer from any form of anxiety. However, those with anxiety will encounter other problems that wouldn't cross other people's minds. It's typical behavior to deny meal invitations from coworkers or friends, ignore unnecessary phone calls, and even avoid small family gatherings. While social situations are more specific and don't occur every day, there are also daily occurrences that can cause extreme amounts of anxiety. For instance, some have issues performing any task or responsibility as long as there's another human being in their presence, looking over their shoulder. We are going to focus on the broader kind of social situation, referring to any environment in which other people are around.

Isolating yourself from any social situation usually leads to more than just personal social isolation. In some cases, this behavior can turn into a never ending cycle of avoidance. The social aspects of life causing you anxiety, can, in turn, create even more tension in new situations. Avoidance reduces your ability to cope, and you will be dealing with even more fear during social gathering. This self-perpetuating cycle often leads to relationship problems, especially breakups, especially if one party is not suffering from any anxiety.

How it Affects your Relationship

Social interactions are more crucial than ever, and if you (or your partner) are suffering from social anxiety, your career and relationships may suffer as a result. Participating in social gatherings and popular events is essential to developing healthy relationships. Building friendships and expanding your career opportunities can almost exclusively be achieved only in a social setting, whether it's an office Christmas party or someone's birthday.

Take a piece of paper or in a journal, write down everything you can remember about your behavior in social situations. Do the same thing for your partner. Here are some of the behavioral clues you may notice that are typical for anyone suffering from social anxiety:

1. Avoiding groups of people by sitting alone at the table, standing in a corner or vanishing for certain periods.
2. Making excuses to leave an event as early as possible.
3. Avoiding the conversation by never getting involved even when offered.
4. Suddenly becoming easily irritated and quick to anger.
5. Consuming more alcohol that what is your normal limit under average circumstances. Many people with anxiety feel they need alcohol to survive a social situation or that they even become more likable.
6. Never leaving the side of your more charismatic and talkative partner.

Consider all of these behaviors and write them down. Writing allows you to process things slower so you can take a deeper look into the various behaviors and reactions. Describe the behavior, feeling, and how you handled the scenario.

Relationship Intimacy Anxiety

Intimacy problems are one of the most common issues relationships encounter. Many couples begin to struggle with sexual activities if they have problems communicating or pre-existing tension that hasn't been worked out and over a prolonged period of stress it can be the reason for a couple to break up. This problem intensifies if anxiety is present.

Let's analyze this situation by starting from the most basic level. The purpose of sex is to produce children that perpetuate the species. Naturally, for the first years, many couples aren't focused on this; however, this doesn't stop human nature. In any case, your body responds to sexual signals and behaviors when you are in a safe place. If you're suffering from constant anxiety, you will need to prepare your mind in such a way that your body relaxes and enough to be ready for a pleasurable intimate experience. You might have to start with various relaxation techniques to place your mind into a safe environment and eliminate all of your thoughts of anxiety.

A variety of reasons cause sexual anxiety, and they are all specific. If you or your partner feel anxious when it comes to sex, it might be due to the following:

1. A past childhood trauma.
2. Lack of confidence and feeling physically unattractive.
3. Past religious beliefs are affecting the way you look at sexual intimacy.
4. Fear regarding your bedroom performance.

How it affects your Relationship

Let's say your partner suffered some kind of sexual trauma in his or her past. This means that being intimate with something is challenging at best, if not impossible. Even well-established relationships that have developed over several years can suffer from the anxiety that this trauma causes. It's good to keep in mind that it's not your fault and you can't put the blame on your partner either. Someone who suffered from a sexual trauma usually requires time, safety and the guidance of a professional therapist in order to navigate these troubled waters. However, undergoing therapy won't solve the problem overnight. On the contrary, if your partner seeks help to explore past issues there may be

an even more significant drop in sexual activity during that time. You should still be careful because if the libido doesn't waiver eventually, it can create a separate issue that affects you both. If you find yourself in this situation, you should sit down with your partner and have an honest discussion about what is happening, or try couple's therapy.

Emotion Control

Remember the last time somebody asked you how you're feeling? You probably answered with "I'm good" or something along those lines, even though you were probably worrying about something or you were angry. We restrain ourselves from being truthful about our feelings because it's the norm. Society doesn't expect us to behave in any other way than what is deemed acceptable. For instance, when you were younger, you probably received a pair of socks or a sweater from someone for your birthday. That probably didn't make you happy or grateful, especially as a kid wanting toys and things to play with. However, you pretended to like it no matter your true feelings because that's how you were supposed to.

How it affects your Relationship

Communication in a relationship can be quite challenging and stressful at times if you or your partner are suppressing your feelings and don't display your genuine\ emotions. The most basic example of this is when you ask your partner what he's angry or upset, and he replies with the classic "I'm fine." Obviously, in this case, it's rather difficult to improve or fix the situation when you can't even get through to your partner. At the same time, however, your partner may also be the type who changes his mood often. Going from one state of mind to another multiple times a week or even a day makes communication even more difficult. Keep in mind a lot of these cases imply the existence of another disorder on top of the anxiety. Also, your partner may occasionally have emotional outbursts or unnecessarily overreact to a situation. In any of these scenarios, communication becomes close to impossible and you might make things worse in the relationship.

Another result of not being able to regulate your emotions has to deal with jealousy and insecurity. For example, if your partner gets suspicious easily and is uncertain about himself. In the case of jealousy, you would have to spend your energy to comforting him and proving nothing is going on, and he shouldn't feel this way. In the case of insecurity, it can be even more exhausting as he will always seek your reassurance on anything, which will test your patience. A sign that both of these issues have in common is clinginess. Whether jealous or insecure, your partner is likely to become clingy and never giving you enough time for yourself. These actions lead to feeling suffocated, a sense of lost identity, and annoyance because you're never alone since you always have to deal with their faults. If you are with someone who can't control his or her emotions, it's easy to feel helpless, and nothing you do is right. Your partner's affliction can easily make you spiral into your very own cycle of anxiety or even depression.

If you are having trouble determining the subtle signs of emotional instability, whether in your partner or yourself, you can work on this exercise to find out. All you need to do is visualize the time when you or your partner felt anxious but without expressing it directly. Write down on a piece of paper the dialogue of that specific situation and the actions taken as a response. That should be a clear sign. You can spend some time thinking of any other cases where anxiety is involved.

Insecure in Love

Insecurities come from the past. Each time your insecurity is triggered, you are reliving past events that are holding you back. It's time to move forward and make peace with the past in order to live a happy, fulfilled life with your loved one. The path to achieving a healthy relationship is not an easy one, and it will take time, effort and persistence. We explained how to recognize your insecurities, what are they and where are they coming from. Understanding all the aspects of your insecurity is an important part of moving forward. Without understanding, you wouldn't be able to make the first steps and invest effort in getting better. Bringing your insecurities to your awareness is already doing wonders, if nothing else, then in motivating you to fight them. Insecurities come as subconscious fears, parts of our defensive mechanisms, tricks and traps of our mind that are holding us back. It is hard to be actively aware, especially in stressful situations and in those first moments when insecurity is triggered. But now you can be aware that it is your inner critical voice speaking; it is not the real you. It's a distorted perception of yourself that is playing with your emotions, using your insecurities to deepen the fear and defend you from being hurt. These defensive mechanisms were useful when we were infants and children. They got stuck with us in adulthood, but now they are bringing more harm than help, and it's time to overcome them.

With the understanding that the problem of your relationship lies in your own insecurities, you should now be aware that not just your thought pattern, but your behavior needs to change too. Your reactions to triggering situations are as harmful as your insecurity, which is undermining you to be happy in a loving, long lasting relationship. But before you try to make any change, what you need is motivation. As mentioned earlier, core beliefs cannot be changed. They have been with us through most of our lives and they are here to stay. The pain that comes with them is something we are often unable to overcome, it's a building block part of your personality. We should not focus on eliminating these beliefs altogether or the pain that comes with them. Instead we should learn how to properly and in a healthy way respond to them when they are triggered.

Acceptance and Commitment therapy (ACT) is making a difference between types of pain we feel when our core beliefs are triggered. First, we recognize primary pain and it is a pain that is unavoidable; the pain we feel we can't control and is a part of us. Secondary pain is the type of pain we create when trying to avoid and control the primary one. Secondary pain influences the behaviors that are ruining our relationship, and this is the pain that we can control and overcome. You need to learn how to control the things that you have control over, and how to accept the things you can't control. To change one's behavior is a difficult task, but it can be done. All you need are valid reasons that will compel you to push forward.

Learn to Accept

What you've been doing wrong thus far is that you put your effort into controlling your core belief. While doing so, you created new pains that pushed you into behaviors that are harming your relationship. You might have isolated yourself, felt uncontrollable anger, or tried to control others. Your efforts to control the uncontrollable pain were hurting you more and more. It's time to consider changing your tactics. Instead of fighting, it is much healthier to allow yourself to feel all the negative emotions that come when your core belief is triggered. It is time to stop fighting and accept defeat in order to be able to transform. It is hard to accept the defeat, and even harder to understand that you need to feel the pain. But if you do this, you will also feel relieved because you won't have to put all the emotional effort needed when battling an enemy, you can't defeat. All the useless struggles you went through trying to control your core belief will go away. The pain will remain, but now that you don't have to fight it, you can listen to it and you might learn something from it.

It might be hard to come to peace with the amount of change you have to go through; the amount of control you need to be able to accept the pain that is a part of you. It might be helpful to think of your painful experience as temporary because it is just that. Think that the situation will go away, but the consequences of your struggles to fight the pain will stay and hurt you even more and create problems in your relationship. When experience that triggers our insecurity is observed as just temporary, it becomes easier to let it go and not react to the experience. We will feel pain, but not reacting to it will give us the calm and objectiveness to repair the damage in our relationship. Put a metaphor in the situation that triggers your core beliefs. It's a storm, the emotions are pretty violent and it puts us in a turmoil, but all storms pass and so will this one. After the storm, sunshine and calm will allow us to repair what's broken and clean the mess that the situation-storm left behind. Do you think you are capable of just letting the storm die out on its own? Negative thoughts we have will always reappear. We can fight them and drive them away for some time, but they will always come back. So, what's the point in being persistent with a strategy that obviously doesn't work? Instead of fighting or avoiding your negative thoughts, try making them helpful. Understand them and accept that they will bring uncontrollable pain, but now you have the strength to experience it and be wiser about it. You are now aware that once the pain goes away, you will be left with much more strength to deal with relationship problems in a much healthier way.

There is a meditation exercise you can do to help you accept the pain caused by your core beliefs:

Sit or lie down comfortably in a place that is very relaxing and where you won't be disturbed by others. Close your eyes and imagine you are a river, water passing by. When thoughts and emotions emerge, imagine them as twigs and leaves carried by the river. Let them pass your vision. You are aware of them for what they are, you are visualizing their temporality as water (you) is carrying them, letting them pass. Even those thoughts and emotions that aren't negative, let them pass. The point of this exercise is to learn how to recognize them for what they are and let go. If you start obsessing over one thought, or one emotion, remember that you are a mighty river and you have the ability to let them go downstream.

Now that you have learned how to recognize and accept your instabilities, you are able to do even more to get rid of them. If not completely, as we learned some of them are imprinted on us as core beliefs, then you will learn how to manage them so they don't hurt your relationship.

Live by Your Values

As we all have imprinted core beliefs, insecurities, we also have imprinted values, characteristics we found useful and that make us happy. These are imprinted on us by our parents, society, and the culture we live in. They are based on morals, personal, and by the society where we grew up. Values vary in different parts of the world, and they can seem pretty personal. It is important to recognize the values you have so you can consciously decide to live by them. Here is a short list of values: Duty, fun, commitment, confidence, affection, clarity, enthusiasm, honor, courage, family, creativity, imagination, freedom, pleasure, loyalty, teamwork, truth, virtue, openness, security, sexuality, wisdom, peace.

These are only some of the possibilities of values. Concentrate and make a list of your values, things that you appreciate the most in others and in yourself.

When our insecurities are triggered by a situation, we have no control over, we might behave opposite of our values; we might even surprise ourselves with our behavior and think "This is not me, this is not how I normally behave." That is true. If you don't want that behavior to be part of you, all you need to do is get rid of it. We can't control situations that will trigger us, life is such and they will happen whether we want them. But what we can control is our reaction to them and how we behave. This will stop us from hurting ourselves even more and stop us from hurting our loved ones.

So, go ahead and write down your values, be aware of the person you want to become and make a commitment to become that person. Make a promise to yourself that your behavior will reflect your values rather than your

Insecurities.

To your value, write down the way how you plan to practice that value:

Openness	Reveal a story from your past to your partner that he or she never heard before
Imagination	Surprise your partner with imaginative and creative dates.
Involvement	Show your partner how much you care by getting involved in his hobbies, family, or anything that he finds important.

Once you manage to replace your negative reactions and behaviors, your relationship will improve significantly, but do not expect it to eliminate all the pain. Remember that pain is coming from a core belief that is imprinted in us and as such we don't have control of it. With exercise and patience, you will come to accept it and manage it in a way that is healthy for both you and your relationship.

Negative Thoughts, How They Influence Us and How to Overcome Them

Negative thoughts come from our core beliefs and as such they will never go away. There are people who always seem positive, and it is true they might be more positive than others, but that is due to their own system of core beliefs. There is no such person who doesn't have negative thoughts. We all are victims of our insecurities. They are either better in managing their responses to negative thoughts or their core beliefs are completely different. They might be the lucky ones who grew up in a safe, loving environment but if you ask them, they, too, have insecurities and negative thoughts to some degree.

Negative thoughts are cognitive barriers that your relationships are dealing with. When you make progress and turn from insecurities-driven negative behaviors to those driven by your values, you will still find yourself dealing with negative thoughts. If you want to learn how to manage them in a way that won't hurt your relationship, you will have to understand what they are and how they work.

Dominate Yourself in Love to Overcome the Fear of Abandonment and Codependent Relationship

In a normal relationship, it is natural for the individuals involved to depend on one another. However, a codependent relationship is different. It is not like the dependency you see in a healthy relationship.

What does a healthy relationship look like?

We are social beings and have been living in groups relying on one another for our survival, food and shelter. It is therefore not wrong to need others and rely on them when you need help. This type of healthy dependency is termed as interdependency.

The normal dependent relationship is a healthy one where there is mutual sharing of support, help and encouragement.

But in a codependent relationship, there is gross imbalance. One person keeps sacrificing for the other without receiving anything in return.

This is a toxic relationship that results in burnout, dissatisfaction and resentment.

In a healthy interdependent relationship, there is enhanced self-esteem, mutual respect, confidence, master and emotional security.

The help, support and encouragement you get from your partner will help you feel safe and confident in tackling any issues you face. It will allow you to overcome any fear and help you grow as an individual.

Thus, there is a perfect balance of independence and dependence. The healthy interdependence does not prevent you from forging ahead and provides you the prop you need for improving yourself.

In an interdependent relationship, the persons involved will feel competent and express their needs. They accept help from others but do not depend on them to improve their self-esteem.

In a codependent relationship, the codependent person is not aware of who he or she is, what they want and how to live as a separate identity.

In short, in a normal and healthy interdependent relationship your identity is not compromised. You can receive and give help while retaining your autonomy and individuality.

Why is codependency unhealthy?

In a codependent relationship, there is over-dependence of one person on another. You feel your identity is fully intermeshed with that of your partner.

Your focus is to such a magnitude that your goals, interests and needs are ignored or suppressed.

While you may hold a job and are capable of paying bills and taking care of your children, you have this unhealthy desire to feel needed.

This desire makes you dependent so you can stay feeling lovable and worthy.

Self-worth for a codependent is based on fixing, helping and rescuing others. This causes an imbalance in the relationship.

Only when both individuals involved accept their roles of giver and taker can the codependent relationship work.

However, it is not at all healthy to sacrifice your needs to feel valued and accepted. This is because the unworthy and flawed feeling creates toxic dependency where you always look to others to validate your beliefs, interests and your existence.

The need or craving to be wanted can leave you trapped in an unhappy, unfulfilling and abusive relationship. Without the caregiver role, you will feel unloved and purposeless.

Enabling is different from helping

In a healthy interdependent relationship, there is mutual support and help where each person has room to grow.

A codependent relationship on the other hand has one person as enabler, doing or rescuing things for the other instead of helping the partner to do things on their own.

The craving for being needed is very powerful and it unconsciously makes you an enabler. The enabled partner will be dependent and dysfunctional as if they are healthy, sober or employed, you will lose your purpose of taking care of them. Without the purpose you will feel unworthy.

This triggers you into acting in such a way that you persistently nag, give unnecessary advice and enable. Helping and enabling differ as helping encourages you to become confident and self-sufficient.

Codependency affects growth

Unlike an interdependent relationship where the people involved are encouraged to grow in all aspects including professional, emotional, spiritual and social, codependent relationship is abusive and unhealthy.

This is because the relationship concentrates on maintaining an imbalance where the giver can go on giving and gain self-esteem by enabling, while the taker has his financial, emotional and physical needs met.

Codependent persons will find it very difficult to function independently due to their self-worth issues and their consistent need to rely on others.

While relationship is vital to your existence adding joy and satisfaction to your life, it cannot fix the underlying wounds in you that you carry into a relationship.

You replay the dysfunctional relationship dynamics and worsen the relationship until the root cause is healed.

Understanding codependency and interdependency

It is difficult to recognize the difference between interdependent and codependent relationship, if you have never been exposed to a normal and healthy relationship.

Here is a table from Webster University on differences between the two relationships. The table will help you clear any doubts you have regarding the nature of your relationship or how a normal and healthy one can look like.

Although the differences between the two relationships are clear, you may still not be able to recognize you are in a codependent relationship that easily.

You have to put in real effort to reflect on your situation and be honest with your feelings. Even if you become aware of the relationship, refraining from such behavior is a difficult task one that needs perseverance and strong will to break the chain and get help to heal and resume a normal and healthy relationship.

Toxic Relationship

There are some situations that breed toxic relationships. They include:

- when a person gets into a relationship with an individual who has an entirely different lifestyle from theirs which does not align in any way.
- when a person gets into a relationship with an individual that has a lousy personality.

Coming up with a final decision to leave an unhealthy relationship may come with feelings of guilt, especially when you've spent longer than necessary with a toxic person. Like we have stated numerous times, toxic relationships are the hardest to recover from even after you have broken up. However, the instant you can free yourself from the feelings of self-blame and self-guilt, you'll experience total well-being and happiness.

The recovery phase after the relationship has ended is one of the most challenging stages you will deal with. For many, it is even more difficult than leaving the toxic relationship because of all the abuse they must have endured during the relationship.

For this reason, we will be delving into a few steps that you need to take if you want to reclaim your self-confidence, dignity, and self-esteem. Below are a few of them.

Detach from Your Toxic Partner Completely

A great move to make after ending a relationship to ensure you heal fast is to stop contacting your former partner. The same is also the case in a toxic relationship. After you have ended the relationship, you need to make sure that you cut all forms of communication with your ex-partner.

Toxic people are very good at manipulation, and if you contact them, you may be tricked into changing your mind and going back to them. Cutting them off is vital because, at this stage, you are still in search of closure and require answers for the things you did wrong. This is the case even when you know you won't get any substantive response. Also, even after the breakup, you will still feel some vulnerability for your former toxic partner. You have to continuously remind yourself of how you got here in the first instance. Do not make yourself available to be abused once more. You need to act like you and your former toxic partner are in different parts of the world. Your ex would do all they can to open the communication lines with you once more. Make sure you block all their phone numbers and make yourself unavailable for them to reach you.

Avoid contacting them through phone calls or social media channels and block them if need be. Disengage entirely from the toxic individual as this will help you heal faster. Ensure you move as far as you can away from them regardless of how difficult it may seem. If you both had kids together, you might need the assistance of an experienced intermediary if you need to contact them. If this is impossible, search for a therapist with the right qualifications to put together a parenting plan for you. This is a legally binding document that consists of all the data about financial obligations and time-sharing for children. It should also include accepted ways for both parties involved to communicate. This will help make the process even more straightforward.

Work Towards Being a Better You

You're free from constantly being pulled down or being told what to do or what not to do. So, you should start learning to work on yourself and let people know the new you through your actions and words. Do only what makes you happy and understand that you should make decisions and do things because of you and not because of anyone else.

Cleanse Your Mind, Body, and Soul of Negativity

A toxic relationship is just like an unhealthy meal. When you eat such a meal, you'll be affected, and your chance of falling ill is very high. So, free your mind, body, and soul of such toxicity. Be positive in every sense of the word by taking part in activities that'll make you happy. You can cleanse your mind by exercising, sightseeing, going out, or being a part of group therapy. If you love singing, writing or dancing, please do so! Just do anything to achieve a mind filled with positivity.

Do Things That'll Boost Your Confidence

Constant belittling and abuse will most likely make you lose your confidence. The more your toxic partner put you down, the more you lose your self-worth and confidence. You've also come to believe you can't do without your partner as they constantly make you feel worthless. To prove to yourself that they've been very wrong about you, you need to build your self-confidence by doing things you're afraid of doing. Are you afraid of public speaking? Why not start by contributing to talk therapy and improve as you gain your confidence back.

Be confident in your decision-making, career goals, and all other things you need to do without looking for validation from anyone. Tell yourself, "I've got this", and do great things that'll surprise you. Most importantly, be confident about your body and yourself and recovering from a toxic relationship will become easier!

Surround Yourself with Positive People

One key feature of a toxic individual is pessimism. While trying to move on from a toxic relationship may be hard, don't make it harder by hanging around negative people. Instead, surround yourself with as much positive energy as possible. You don't want to leave an abusive relationship and get abused again. If this happens, it means you haven't learned from you just experience. Move with people that are ready to bring out the best in you and support you always. Your friends understand that you're trying to heal and if they love you, they'll help you through this period.

Enjoy Your Own Company

If you don't love yourself, how then will people love you? When you learn to enjoy being alone, you'll discover something new about yourself and love yourself more. Being alone shouldn't amount to loneliness; instead, it should be a time to meditate and reflect on your life and what to do to make yourself happy.

As soon as you're able to understand this, it becomes easy to move on, and you don't have to be scared of being lonely. You will also discover that being alone offers you peace, and you're happier than being with an abusive partner.

Try to Love Again

If you don't want to love again after leaving an abusive partner, it's understandable! Due to your experience with a toxic partner, you may find it hard to love again. But there's someone out there dying to be with someone like you. You deserve to be loved and should not deny yourself the opportunity of experiencing a healthier and happier relationship. Whenever you're ready to date, ensure that you watch out for signs of toxicity in people you meet to avoid repetition. Be very sure that you're prepared to move on before you decide to do so.

Narcissistic Relationship

What is it and How Recognize It?

Whether or not you feel like you have been the victim of narcissistic abuse, being in a relationship with a narcissist is not without its challenges and may lead to an unhappy end, or rather, it could lead to you staying in it, even when it contradicts who you are as a person and your dreams and goals of successful relationships and a happy life. Whatever you are feeling at this moment as you read this, letting go of your relationship may not feel like your first choice, and that's okay.

If you feel like you need to stay in your relationship in order to ask yourself more questions, then you can return to help you continue to identify patterns of behavior or symptoms of abuse. You may need to spend more time reflecting on the issues in your relationship from a more objective standpoint for a little longer, before you answer to these about letting go and moving on.

For some readers, there is no question that it is time to pack up and go. It all depends on a person's wants and needs and their ability to be honest with the truth of what is really going on in their marriage or partnership. It can take some time to understand the dynamics of your narcissistic partnership after you have identified that you are in one.

Moving forward can be a challenge and many people will struggle with putting an end to this type of relationship, mainly due to the reality of narcissistic abuse and emotional manipulation. It really is about who you are, what your experience is and what is going on right now that will help you understand the best choice forward for you.

The following will help you identify when it might be good to leave a narcissistic relationship and how to put an end to it so that you don't keep coming back to it and repeating the same patterns repeatedly. A lot of that experience requires getting help and support and eventually a period of recovery from the narcissistic relationship so that you don't end up with the same type of person again, repeating the patterns in an entirely new relationship.

Recover Yourself from Emotional Abuse and Manipulation

Therefore, trying to change a narcissist and help, they work on growth and transformation is not going to get you very far. If you are trying to stick around and make it work, the best possible advice is to just try to focus on their positive qualities. Even if your narcissist claims that they want to change, there will be little effort put forth and very little gain. They aren't going to be able to offer a change in the way that you are needing or hoping and you will most often find yourself alone emotionally. You want to heal them, but only they can heal themselves and so you might be waiting for a long time for them to find that out.

The time is right for you to leave if you have undergone any emotional, mental or physical abuse, if you have identified serious cycles of manipulation or narcissistic issues that never change, if you are sacrificing your own personal power, integrity, success and desires, or if you feel like you are being taken advantage of on a regular basis to support someone else's fantasies of who they are. There are a lot of ways that narcissism from within your relationship can affect your quality of life, your personal views, your self-worth and more, and it is not worth it to stick around hoping that your partner will change and be more what you need. They don't care about what you need. They will only ever care about what they need.

If you have tried for a long time to help your partner identify their issue and help them "heal" their problem to no avail, then it is time to let go and move on. It is important to recognize that you can never heal someone for them; they have to do the work to heal themselves. Being a supportive partner is always a good thing, but if you are familiar with how your patterns of support have enabled your narcissistic partner to stay in their preferred role and behavior patterns, then you need to admit that you are at the end the rope so that you can heal on your own terms and find a happier lifestyle.

The stages of detaching from your partner can go on for a while as you begin to identify the issues and start to pull away, changing your role in the situation and recognizing your readiness to end things. It can be uncomfortable for your partner, who will make it uncomfortable for you as a result, and so understanding some of the stages that you will likely go through will help you prepare for moving on.

Take Revenge from Your Toxic Relationship

First Stage:

When the rose-colored glasses come off, and you stop accepting blame, guilt or shame in your relationship, you begin to resurface and "wake-up" to what has really been going on. In the first stage, you are "seeing" more clearly all of the patterns, the covert and subversive ridicule, and all of the tools of manipulation to push you away and punish you, and then pull you back in and adore you. This is the stage of awareness of the problem and the first shift and change of the situation.

Second Stage:

You may still have feelings for your partner at this point, even a seriously deep love bond, however, your usual desire to please them no matter what will begin to be replaced with the feeling of anger, and even resentment that they are so consistently and continuously demanding of your admiration, adoration and pleasing them. The love may still be there, but you are not so "naïve" anymore.

Signals of the Second Stage:

- Your partner's lies no longer have an effect on you and feel obvious and pathetic.
- You are no longer succumbing to the manipulation tools.
- You regain a sense of self-worth and feel you deserve to be treated better.
- You will begin to fight for yourself more and will create more conflict with your partner.
- You begin to regain and rebuild your self-confidence and self-esteem.

Third Stage:

Your confidence is being reborn and you are feeling better about yourself and your choices. You may have already joined a support group at this time, or started to see a counselor to help your growth, and are feeling more empowered emotionally and mentally. You can better focus on your own wants and needs and can start to see how life would be if you are not involved with your narcissistic partner.

Signals of the third stage:

- You cannot stand to be around your partner.
- You no longer feel an obsessive love or strong love bond.
- If they begin to push your buttons or act inappropriately, you will either have no reaction and not care, or retaliate and lash out against them.
- Enjoying more time with friends, in support groups, engaging in classes or group meet-ups that support your interests
- You will start to make decisions to support yourself without concerning yourself with your partner's preferences or interests.
- You will begin to make your move to let go and move on by planning your life out.

Fourth Stage:

This is the end of the relationship when your focus becomes facing your future without your partner. At this point, you may have cut the cords, moved out, separated, begun the divorce proceedings, etc. This is the stage when you will have cut them off and out of your life and when you can begin to feel new and like yourself again. You will not want anything to do with your partner and in some cases; you may have to maintain some kind of contact (if you have children together).

The Overall Process of Letting Go and Moving On:

This process won't occur for anyone overnight. You can end up living in the cycles of one stage for a long time until you are resolved to move forward. Being stuck in these processes is highly common and there is a way to help you ease through a little bit better so that you don't stay stuck for longer than you need to be.

Section III – More Important Section

Understanding How Not to Attract People with Personality Disorder

Before we address some advice for dealing with a narcissist and the aftermath of abuse, it is important that we outline some of the key indicators that you are indeed suffering from narcissistic abuse syndrome.

The first and foremost signal to yourself that you are suffering from dealing with a narcissist in a toxic relationship is the persistent feeling that you are alone. If you come home each day and see your boyfriend, eat meals with your boyfriend, sit in front of a TV with your boyfriend, then go to bed to a boyfriend, but still feel like you've spent the whole day alone, it's because you might be dealing with a narcissist who is only presenting to you a mirage of the relationship you thought you were living. There is an absence of feeling underneath the actions that leave you feeling lost, confused, and very lonely. If you feel this constantly and are unsure of where the feeling came from, this may be a sign of narcissistic abuse syndrome.

If you are constantly struggling with the feeling that you are just not good enough for anyone, especially your boyfriend/partner, then you may be suffering from narcissistic abuse syndrome. Narcissists are very good at tearing down their victims' self-esteem and convincing them through both subtle and not-so-subtle strategies that they are messing things up, constantly making mistakes, etc. They may make fun of you and laugh at you or mock you and make you feel small. This abuse leads you to believe that you are worthless and that you would never be good enough for anything you want to accomplish in life.

You may feel suffocated by the relationship itself as your narcissist partner attempts to hijack your personal life and everything that existed before he/she entered your life. It is a trademark strategy of exercising control to isolate the victim from those he/she once trusted and loved. It is the narcissist's goal to make him/herself the only person you lean on for anything kind of support.

Another sign of narcissistic abuse syndrome is the realization that you've become a different person in terms of belief systems, morals, principles, or other characteristics that were once at the core of who you are. If your partner has managed to change these essential things about you and they don't seem right, it is a sign that you've got some toxic forces at work doing everything they can to make you into a different person that serves the purposes of only the narcissist.

Narcissists often utilize outright name-calling in an effort to belittle and gradually break down a victim's sense of self-worth. This practice may not be overt in the beginning, but instead, be framed as a kind of joke and kidding by the narcissist. He may say while giggling, "You're just overreacting because you're too sensitive." Comments like these may seem innocent at first, but over time with persistent use, these things can be internalized by the victim until the accusations became a reality for them. They may start to believe these things which at first, they didn't feel were affecting them in any damaging way.

Finally, the cycle of something called "hurt and rescue" can take such a toll on a victim as to lead to life-long emotional anxieties and struggles. With this technique, the narcissist introduces stress through an event or an argument or an accusation and then gives the victim the silent treatment for a certain amount of time. They may use a tactic other than the silent treatment, but whatever they choose to do, the object is to relieve that stress or silence it for an amount of time. The silent treatment, when used in this way, triggers a fear of abandonment that is innate in pretty much every human being out there. This makes it an inescapable strategy to induce pain, as long as the victim feels attachment and emotion for the perpetrator.

The rescue stage entails the perpetrator coming back and relieving that fear of abandonment, but now, the victim has learned to be afraid whenever the cycle starts again, anticipating that period of staged abandonment, or silence.

Over time, this technique becomes a powerful strategy for control and manipulating behaviors because the feelings associated with abandonment can be so strong and hurtful. Each one of us is hardwired to crave attention, love, and affection, so when someone offers this then abruptly takes it away, we learn to do whatever we need to do to avoid having that attachment leave us again, even if it means apologizing for something we didn't even do, much to the narcissist's delight.

When you feel sure you are dealing with a narcissist in a romantic relationship, you need to seek support in getting out and away as soon as possible. Educate yourself on the tactics used by narcissists to keep that feeling of attachment in you and do everything you can to resist it and break free. Remind yourself again and again that it's all been an act and nothing you were feeling attached to is real.

If you are dealing with a narcissist who is not a romantic partner but still an unavoidable part of your life, your best defense is going to be constant awareness and alertness to any schemes and manipulation the narcissist may be trying to employ on you. It would be unwise to start an all-out war on the narcissist since his whole being is centered on crushing others and he will surely be able to invest more time and emotional energy into hurting you than you will in hurting him. Besides, you're not that kind of person!

Even though you may feel anger, letting your guard down and losing control is exactly what the narcissist wants you to do, so do not give him the satisfaction.

As always, strength in numbers is a good rule of thumb to follow. If you are feeling vulnerable or susceptible to a narcissist in your purview, recruit others to support you and help form a barrier. Let the narcissist know that you are too smart to fall for his schemes and that you are not going to give an inch. Create a thick skin around yourself and prepare for some demeaning insults designed to rile you up. You don't have to give in to these. Form your support group and move on with your life. When the narcissist sees that you've all but become immune to his charms, he will look elsewhere and leave you alone. Be on the lookout for others whom he may be targeting and be sure to let them know what's going on if you think they are also in danger. This will probably trigger a defensive response, but the key is to maintain your composure and remind yourself of your reality and your standing. Don't buy into the narcissist portraying himself as more than what he is. Inside, he is just an insecure little boy trying to validate himself through other people's praises. He does not have power over you or those you love. You are stronger than this person because you know the strength and power of genuine love and affection.

We will discuss some advice and tips for those who have gone through the abuse from a narcissist and are on the journey towards recovery. We will also discuss how you can arm yourself against future narcissist abuse. As always, I encourage you to educate yourself as much as possible about the narcissist and his various schemes. Knowledge, after all, is power.

Section III: Couples Communication

Couples Communication

It is quite unfortunate that the importance of communication is often not taken seriously in marriage. This is mainly because so many couples think daily banter or lack thereof does not affect them every day.

However, you must understand that communication is the engine that fuels all other parts of a marriage. If you love your spouse and fail to show them through words and actions, then the truth is that you are not doing right by them. If you genuinely love and trust them, then let them know how you feel about them. Communicating openly and with honesty ensures that your marriage stands a chance of flourishing and staying healthy. Communication must begin right from the time you are courting to marriage and into marriage.

When you and your husband or wife make effective communication the cornerstone of your marriage, you will enjoy a loving marriage. The only shortcoming is that there are people who are just not good at it. Having love, honesty, and trust is good, but they are not meaningful by themselves. It is by expressing these traits that yield a marriage that will become the envy of many.

The magic lies in showing love, acting honestly, and showcasing trust. Communicating how much your husband or wife means to you moves your marriage from good to high! The point is, expressing yourself goes beyond words alone.

Advice and Proven Strategies

Some of the benefits associated with effective communication in marriage include;

It Minimizes Confusion

Did you know that when you have been married to someone for 50+ years, you still cannot predict what is going through their mind? One of the biggest mistakes that couples today make is assuming that their spouse "knows." The problem with this kind of assumption is that your spouse may be thinking a complete opposite of what you thought at first.

According to Eboni Baugh and Deborah Humphreys (Extension specialists at the University of Florida), it is critical that you clearly state your thoughts with utmost honesty to minimize confusion. Additionally, when saying your thoughts, do it positively as much as you can.

When you minimize confusion, what you are doing is increasing the commitment in your relationship. This commitment is what is directly related to satisfaction in marriage.

It Maintains Marriages through Assurances

Satisfaction in relationships is directly correlated to the assurance that you give your partner. Marianne Dainton, a communications researcher, explains that assurance in marriage is what reaffirms you're the romantic desires of your partner. You can achieve this by choosing to use kind words and acts of love.

Other researchers report that couples who often engage in assurances often enjoy more significant commitment in their marriage which impacts positively on their marital satisfaction.

It Enhances Marital Satisfaction

As we have already said, it is evident that when communications are effective in marriage, then couples can enjoy marital satisfaction. When you are satisfied with your marriage, you will live a healthier life, and this will increase your lifespan significantly.

However, if you are in a marriage that is characterized by poor communications, you will likely be caught up in a vicious cycle of poor, unhealthy conversations that contribute to dissatisfaction. When this cycle of poor communication is not corrected early enough, it has a likelihood of degrading your relationship.

It Keeps a Couple Closer than they Think

How do you know your spouse for who they are? Is there a way to know? One thing that you need to bear in mind is that no one has a premonition or the power to read other's minds. When we share our life's stories and experiences, we are certainly going to involve ourselves with others.

The same thing applies to marriage. Marriage is not just about physical contact; it is also about having an emotional connection with another. When you share a little experience from your life with someone however small it may be, this form of openness will surely draw you nearer to one another. It is what makes you both feel like one.

The only way you are going to know what is going through your spouse's mind and heart is by asking them. This is one of the best ways to resolve any issues that arise in a fast and effective way possible.

Assumptions and Misunderstandings are Likely Not to Creep In

One of the things that we have mentioned earlier is that of making assumptions. But the most critical question is, how does communication in marriage ensure that assumptions and misunderstanding do not creep in?

Well, one thing that we have to note is that it is natural for one's mind to wander off and have the worst thoughts possible when they feel that their spouse is not sharing some specific information.

Think about a situation where you and your significant other speak to each other without any inhibitions. Will there be any form of negativity? Certainly not! The main reason is that you are ensuring that you close the door for assumptions. This way, you eliminate negativity out of your life.

Once you know what you both like and dislike beliefs, desires, opinions, and wants in life, you both will likely decide to see your marriage through to success. But the question is, "what do you think is holding you back?" Well, when you open your heart to someone else, this is indeed a blessing. The main reason is that you know that there is someone in this life that knows and appreciates you for who you truly are.

Therefore, ensure that you are not keeping verbal gaps between the two of you to avoid the occurrence of disappointments and feelings of insecurities.

Learn to Improve Your Skills and Eliminating Conflicts

Reduce the Occurrence of Infidelity

Now, let's take a look at communication from a different angle. Ask yourself what communicating with others lead to. When did your spouse fail to share things with you that can be interpreted as not sharing their life with you, right?

Well, it is important to note that when you keep things from your spouse or even avoid a major conversation/argument and desiring to be left alone play a central role in breaking the bond that you share. In other words, when you do this, you are pushing your spouse away.

In as much as this may not be the same case for all couples, lacking an emotional connection with your spouse may arouse the desire to make a connection with someone else. Trust me, you may not want to go down this path, but when your heart is not fulfilled with all of its needs and desires, it will strive to bring itself that satisfaction it wants.

Demonstrate Respect for your Spouse through Honesty

Have you ever found yourself in a situation where you do not wish to talk to your spouse, or your spouse does not want to talk to you and hence end the conversation right there and then?

Well, the truth is that this may work for you at least once or twice. However, over time, you may need to add in a few lies just so that you can get out of the situation. Note that, at this point, it is no longer avoidance; it is now backed up with a pack of lies!

Now, the most important thing you need to note is, when there is nothing to hide from your significant other, there is no need to introduce false information. What this does is that it destroys the chances of you having a beautiful life you have always wanted with your spouse.

At first, it may start as an innocent thing to keep stuff from your spouse. However, with time, it is this kind of behavior that highlights your lack of respect for them. It is high time that you become honest with them at least that is what you owe them. They need to know what is going on in your life, mind, and heart so that you can both handle the situation and get ahead with life.

That said, you have to bear in mind that communication in marriage or any other relationship for that matter is a two-way street without any red lights. When you are communicating with your spouse, it is much more than just sharing what you both have in mind. You cannot drop your frustrations, anger, and news at your spouse and then walk away like nothing just happened.

Understand that communicating simply means that you have to be present for each other. You have to be there when your spouse needs you to comfort them both physically and emotionally. Get over the belief that as a couple, you just say what you feel and walk out of the room.

Opening yourself to your spouse means that you welcome the possibility of receiving information from them as well. In life, whether marriage or elsewhere, we all desire to be needed and wanted by someone. When you are there for each other in marriage, you will be able to face problems and issues together. Nothing will be tough for you. There will be no argument big enough to threaten to break your relationship.

Indeed, communication is a process, but the most important thing is to learn that process so that it can bring you and your spouse closer. When you both learn how to communicate with each other, you develop a unique language. This is not to say that the process of learning effective communication is easy!

Importance of Counseling Before Marriage

If you are not yet married and are reading this, bravo! This is a great step when preparing to get married. One thing that you have to understand is that marriage is an exciting engagement that is often followed by a range of plans and activities for the wedding.

At this point, much of the details of your communication may take a focus on the wedding. If you are not careful, the wedding may take the place of even much more important discussions about your future as a married couple. When you seek marriage counseling ahead of your marriage, you are simply increasing your chances of enjoying a satisfying union together. Yes, you may have fallen in love with each other, but you have to understand that a happily ever after takes lots of effort and preparation!

Commitment

One of the primary benefits of seeking marriage counseling is showing how committed you are to the success of your marriage. It is through premarital counseling that a couple is offered an opportunity to plan how they will journey through marriage together as an entity. Most importantly, counseling before marriage offers you and your spouse-to-be an opportunity to develop critical problem-solving strategies together.

Realize that when you come into a marriage with the expectation that every plan will fall in place is only a recipe for disaster. There is a difference between walking blindly and expecting the best but also knowing how to handle situations when the worst happens. It is critical always to have a backup plan in case you both fall into moments of crises so that you can handle issues with so much hope and humor. This way, you protect your marriage from stress and dissatisfaction.

Relationship Questions for Couples

"Where are we headed as a couple?"

This set of questions concerns your future trajectory as a pair. Each is designed to facilitate a discussion that is more firmly grounded in reality than the conversations prompted, which featured a lot of speculative and abstract desires. You might want to think of the difference in these terms was about planning a dream vacation that you'd take someday in the hypothetical future with an unlimited budget, then by contrast, this is asking you to plan an actual trip, this year, funded by the money you currently have in the bank.

Don't feel any pressure to get through all these questions in one session or even all in one week. Your collective future deserves deep thought and consideration. If any of these questions expose a disparity, in terms of what you're each expecting from your future together, take some time to discuss the issue. How important is this goal to each of you, and how flexible can you be? Is this an instance wherein you might work together to design a compromise? Or could you each pursue your own separate goals without pulling too much energy or attention away from the relationship?

In these modern times, there are no road maps or blueprints to adhere to; prescribed gender roles and notions of what a typical couple should look like and how it should operate are changing every day. Don't be afraid to make outlandish suggestions for compromise, or to negotiate powerfully for your own needs in the relationship. Rather than worrying over how your relationship should progress, focus instead on how it does work now, and how it can work even better in the future to serve you both.

- Who is my partner?
- What type of relationship do we have?
- How do we relate to each other?
- What are my personal goals?
- Why do we disagree?

This is a good point to take a little break and check in with yourself. How are you feeling about these answers? Did you notice any similarities in your future personal plans and your collective plans? Or did you find that your partner's few steps are heading in a different direction than you expected?

Neither reality is a foolproof recipe for success or disaster. If you noted lots of differences, you might want to have a purposeful conversation with your partner to find out how you can make space for both of your visions in the relationship.

If your goals are already quite similar, you might want to talk instead about how your relationship will fare if these goals suddenly become unreachable--for instance, if a large percentage of your focus is on building a family together, how might your relationship handle a struggle with infertility or inability to adopt?

Furthermore, in the case that your goals are already aligned, you will each need to make a concerted effort to hold onto your own identities within the relationship. As a society, we tend to romanticize relationships wherein couples spend all of their time together, know each other inside and out, and each partner feels like they could not live without the other, but in reality, these are not healthy ideals to strive for. It's reasonable to perform selfless acts from time to time and make small personal sacrifices to build something great together, but without healthy boundaries, you could easily give too much of yourself to your relationship, and wind up feeling drained or neglected.

If this is a concern of yours, each of you should check your answers from the first set of questions, and determine some firm boundaries for yourselves. For your own benefit, list at least three personal values or goals that you would not be willing to give up, even if your partner pressured you to. If you or your partner has a difficult time recognizing the difference between your personal needs and the needs of the relationship, then professional counseling might be a healthy step.

Remember, setting boundaries is not the same thing as being stubborn or emotionally closed off, insisting on full autonomy or focusing exclusively on your own needs. In any relationship, total independence can be a barrier to intimacy. As you grow to trust one another, it's natural to begin relying on each other for certain things. For example, in a committed relationship, one partner might volunteer to take care of cooking meals if their loved one lacks kitchen skills, or is often busy with work late into the evenings; meanwhile, the other partner might agree to pay for the groceries, or handle the dishwashing after the meal. You might grow to count on your partner in larger ways, too: for emotional support in times of difficulty, or for physical support when you are injured or ill. It's also natural to be somewhat flexible about your boundaries, allowing firm rules to be bent under extreme or fluctuating circumstances.

Healthy couples function interdependently. There is a vast difference between being co-dependent and interdependent. A person who is co-dependent in a relationship may struggle to maintain personal friendships outside the partnership, to identify personal feelings or desires, and have trouble standing up for their own needs if they clash with the needs of their significant other. If you find that you are prioritizing the needs of the relationship over your own well-being, this is a sign that your relationship has become codependent to an unhealthy degree, and you'll want to take some steps to restore balance in the partnership.

A person who has mastered interdependence is comfortable trusting their partner to accommodate some of their needs, but he/she also has a support system in place outside of the relationship. They are able to take time and space away from the relationship without feeling the stability of the relationship might be threatened, and they feel secure in knowing that their personal needs are just as important as the needs of their partner while striving towards collective happiness.

For your partnership to stand the test of time, you'll need to build a strong support system for it. Work to find a balance between shared and independent recreation time. Both of you will need to pursue your own hobbies and passions. It is wise for each of you to have your own friends to turn to in times of need, or when you simply want to blow off some steam. If you plan to share a business, child, or other time-consuming responsibility, make sure that both of you are compromising equally for it, and that you each are given opportunities to take time away from this responsibility.

Best Relationship Activities for Couples

We will look at ways to spice up your sex life with some fun games and challenges you can play, of the erotic variety, of course. Including sexy games and challenges will keep your relationship fun and flirtatious for a long time to come and these you can keep changing and introducing new ones to keep the experimentation alive. You may have played innocently flirtatious games in middle school like spin the bottle or 7 minutes in heaven. We are going to use a similar idea of fun and games but a much less innocent variety. These games are designed for you and your partner to have some sexy fun together. You can use this as foreplay or as fun in the evening. It doesn't have to progress to full-blown sex, but I assure you that you both will be heavily turned on after playing one of these that you will not be able to wait to get to penetration. Just try not to come too early on in the game!

Never Have I Ever

This game is a fun way to learn more about your partner's sexual history, but in turn, they will also learn about yours! Both of you will begin with five fingers up- these represent your lives. One of you goes first and says something they have never done, for example: "Never have I ever had a threesome." If your partner has done it, they have to put down one finger. You go back and forth like this and the first person to lose all of their lives loses the game! The loser will then have to give the winner something of their choosing. This game can also be played as a drinking game where, instead of lives using fingers, if the other person has done the thing you say, they have to take a sip of their drink. If you play this way, it can go on for quite a while since there are no lives. To keep it fun and lighthearted, say things that you have not done, but that is not targeted at the other person such as "never have I ever been named John" if your partner is named John. Keep it fun and sexy by saying things related to dating, sex and all taboo topics you can think of. Play this game with the intention of getting to know your partner better and having them get to know you better as well.

Spin the Bottle

Traditional spin the bottle is done in a large group of people, with each person being an option the bottle can land on. Everyone sits in a circle with the bottle lying on its side in the middle. You spin the bottle on its side and whoever the opening is facing when it stops spinning is the person that you have to kiss.

In this spin on spin the bottle, we are going to switch it up a little bit. You can play this game with anything you have, all you'll need is some type of bottle, some paper, and a pen. Think of the regular spin the bottle circle, with 6 or 8 people all sitting in a circle. Instead of people, we are going to have one challenge at each spot. At each spot, there will be a piece of paper with a challenge written on it, and whichever spot the bottleneck is facing after your spin

- Lick my nipples
- Give me a hickey
- Give me oral sex for 2 minutes

- Pick which position we will have sex in after this game
- Strip down to your underwear
- Give me a massage on a body part of my choosing for 2 minutes
- Give me a lap dance
- Take off my shirt using your teeth
- I will look for the craziest sex position I can find online, and you attempt it with me

Truth or Dare

Play sexy Truth or Dare with your partner. Just like when you were young, a game of Truth or Dare helps you get to know people in a funny and sometimes daring way. If you don't know how to play, I will explain the rules first! Each partner takes a turn asking the other person, "Truth or Dare?" The person responds with their answer, and depending on which they choose, a truth- a question that they have to answer truthfully, or a dare- a challenge that they have to complete, is given to them. If they do not complete the dare or will not answer the truth question, they have to accept a pre-determined punishment. This punishment can be to take a shot (If you are playing a drinking version) or to give you a massage, anything you wish. Decide this punishment at the beginning of the game. As you play, you will make up truths or dares for your partner that get them to tell you or do things to you that are fun and sexy! Below are some examples of truths or dares that you can give them:

Truths:

- Tell me your wildest sexual fantasy
- What did you think about/imagine/ watch last time you masturbated?
- What is your favorite sexual memory?
- What is something you have always wanted to try during sex?
- What is the naughtiest thing you have ever done?

Dares:

- Lick peanut butter off of somewhere on your body of your choosing ex. finger, chest
- Turn the lights off and try to turn the other person on using only sounds
- Do a striptease to a song of your choosing
- Make out with their belly button
- Demonstrate their favorite sex position with a pillow
- Give them a lap dance
- Give them a hickey

Icebreakers:

The Game of Truth

Music Share

Swap Books

Couples Counseling Exercises, Worksheets, & Techniques

Most couples who are faced with major problems in their relationship, don't realize that their relationship demands more effort, work and dedication, until it becomes "too late" to react to progressive conflicts and negative changes. Worksheets and techniques designed for couples who want to get the best out of their relationship are focused on exercising all key factors and qualities that make a relationship functional, happy, and healthy. To help you maintain your relationship and enhance its functionality, we are sharing some of the top worksheets and techniques used in couples' therapy.

Apologizing

We are starting off with perhaps one of the most commonly deserted acts when it comes to resolving conflicts – admitting you are wrong and apologizing for your actions, behavior, bad words, or actions. Saying "I am sorry" and hoping that you would be understood and forgiven is sometimes not enough, especially when it comes to major conflicts and disagreements. Let's say that you or your partner did something horrible, which consequently affected your relationship and the way you see each other. Would a simple "I am sorry" resolve the problem? Most likely no. That is why you need to learn how to apologize in an effective way so that your apology actually matters. An effective apology starts with acknowledging that you did something wrong while also acknowledging and recognizing the fact that your partner is hurt and upset. You need to let your partner know that you are aware of how they feel and that you are also well aware that you are the one responsible for the way they feel. You need to address the problem as well, so your partner would realize that you understand why they are upset and what it is that you did wrong.

This step would be explaining yourself and why you made a mistake that ended up hurting your partner. Whether you intentionally hurt your partner or unintentionally created the problem between you, you need to be honest and come clean while explaining the reason behind your actions.

Self-reflection

Self-reflection is an important part of couple's therapy even though this exercise technique calls for individual work, which means that both partners need to participate in self-reflection, but are due to work on this exercise by themselves and without their partner's presence or influence. This technique is designed to help you find gratitude and appreciation in your relationship and for your partner. We sometimes forget how lucky we are to have someone we love and who loves us back, which can backfire in the form of losing that significant someone. Finding appreciation and gratitude for your partner will help you deepen your relationship as well as reflect on yourself and on everything you give and receive in your relationship. Think about the past week and every experience you had that involved your partner in those last seven days. While reflecting on your week, you need to focus on your relationship with your partner and forget about everything else as the

exercise is in the process. You will create a list that will contain three different categories, each named in the following order:

- What did I receive from my partner?
- What did I give to my partner?
- Did I create a problem and why?
- Did my partner create a problem and why?

Once you arrange the categories of your self-reflection list, you may focus on the past week and answer the questions. For instance, under the first categories, you should write that your partner gave to you in the following week, counting on tokens of attention such as making you a coffee, packing lunch for both of you, letting you know that you are loved and appreciated, and other things that would speak in favor of a healthy relationship. Your partner should work separately on their own self-reflection list, creating the same categories as you have on your list. Under the second category, you should write everything you did for your partner in the past seven days, likewise counting on showing care, appreciation, dedication, commitment, attention, affection, and other positive qualities that describe a

healthy relationship. All couples argue and encounter disagreements every once in a while, so you need to put all disagreements and problems you believe were caused by you in the past week (if any), while the fourth categories should contain same values only in relation to your partner's negative actions and behavior in the past week (if any). While working individually on your self-reflection list should help you perceive the reality of your relationship on a weekly basis, comparing your lists together with your partner will help you understand how each of you perceives your relationship and everyday interactions between the two of you. Raising your own awareness of what you have will help you find gratitude for your partner, while listing negative experiences that took place in the near past should help you work out your problems more efficiently. Remember to be honest and trust your partner to make your relationship work. More importantly, don't take your partner for granted.

Speak Openly, Freely and Honestly

Communication is essential, clear communication is the key to a functional relationship, while speaking openly, freely and honestly will help you reestablish and establish a deep connection and understanding between you and your partner. This exercise is created to help you work on your intimacy and sex life, need for attention and fulfilling your partner's

need for attention, as well as help you with creating a healthy environment for your relationship through communication as the main tool. We have already placed a major emphasis on how important communication in relationships is, and now we are going to present you with an effective way of removing barricades between you and your partner. In case you are struggling with being open about your needs, emotions and thoughts, you are actually creating more opportunities for conflicts, misunderstandings and disagreements. By being open and trusting that your partner will deal with openness in the same way, you are actually establishing a strong basis for your relationship. That way, you may come clean with any problem you think you have as well as show verbal appreciation to your partner.

Take action, communicate, be open, and expressing yourself might as well turn into ultimate fun times. The same goes for any other aspect of your relationship. If you feel like being hugged, you may ask your partner; "Do you want me to hug you?" or "Would you like me to hug you". When it comes to disagreements and hardships, you should as well be brave enough to state your mind and be honest, free and open. When you feel like something has been done wrong to you, and you believe that your partner is directly responsible for the way you feel, you may state your mind and say: "I don't feel that well because…" or "I think that what you did is wrong because…". Be open, free and honest

when it comes to taking the opposite role – in cases where you are the one who's done something wrong.

Accepting Your Partner's Influence

"Old habits die hard" may be true, but when you are a part of a collective such as family, marriage or a relationship, sometimes your habits need to be changed, revised, diminished and transformed. A part of this change of habits and the ways you are acting and reacting to internal and external factors will be mildly or fairly transformed without your awareness as you are sharing a relationship with your partner – however, some of your partner's influences should be accepted intentionally and with full awareness. This exercise is narrowly related to the aspect of decision making in relationships. Decision making in relationships concerns every decision that may influence or affect your relationship, while both partners are due to make this type of decision together and within an agreement. To be able to avoid conflict of interests, arguments and inability to come to an agreement when trying to make a decision together, you and your partner can make a set of rules.

Ritualizing Mundane Things

This exercise is perhaps the most fun by far as you will be able to work together with your partner on creating rituals out of everyday things and activities that you will both follow up with and adopt within an agreement. Both partners may make suggestions on which activities should be shared and ritualized, i.e. done seasonally, daily, weekly, monthly, yearly. Rituals will help you make a deeper connection with your partner through romanticizing everyday activities – these activities will be the anchor of keeping up the positive dynamic in your relationship. You can make a list of all activities you and your partner would like to include. Take a look at our sample list of bonding rituals for couples.

Daily:

- Drinking coffee together in the morning
- Meeting up for lunch
- Having dinner together

Weekly

- Going out
- Sharing a hobby
- Watching your favorite TV show
- Watching a movie
- Cooking dinner together

Monthly

- Go on a romantic getaway weekend
- Double-date night

Annually

- Celebrating your anniversary
- Doing something nice for each other's birthdays

You and your partner may agree to ritualize activities that both of you enjoy and appreciate, which is more than an effective way of connecting with your partner and creating pleasurable milestones on a daily, weekly, monthly and yearly basis.

Relationship Reassessment

Reassessing your relationship and values held in the most important aspects of your relationship with your partner, will help you find out which areas would use improvement

and which areas are working properly. Being aware of weaknesses and strengths in your relationship will help you appreciate all the good things between you and your partner, while helping you develop awareness on everything that needs to be changed in order to improve your relationship. You can easily reassess your relationship by creating a list based on the following pattern:

Wish Lists

Yes, making lists is an extremely effective way of taking the very first steps towards making a positive action, which is why we are making yet another list. You and your partner will once again create separate lists that you will share with each other and discuss the reasons behind your entries. The last worksheet technique in our guide, but not the least, revolves around predicting the future of your relationship as well as letting your partner know what you want your relationship to become and how you see your relationship in the present. Divide your list into two columns, naming one of the columns "Present" and the other "Future". The first column should be divided into two smaller columns that should contain three wishes each.

Present		Future
Positive	Negative	
Write up all the positive things in your	Write up all the negative things you are able to note in your	Make a list of three wishes regarding the future of your

| relationship you are able to note in the present, making a list of three wishes about your relationship in the future | relationship in the present, making three wishes on which negative qualities you would like to see less | relationship |

Exercises for Couples

Exercise 1: the 3-minute rule

Sometimes there is an imbalance in the couple, especially when one doesn't dare to express himself while the other is a real chatterbox! The aim of this exercise is to give the floor in an equitable manner, in 3-minute increments. Choose a subject that causes regular tension in your relationship. One of you starts to speak, at random, and he or she is entitled to his or her 3 minutes to say everything that is on his or her mind without being interrupted. Then it's the other's turn.

Everyone must express their point of view without aggression, and in a constructive way. The process is to be continued until the subject is settled. If, despite several constructive proposals, the problem seems unsolvable, pause and take a step back. Repeat the exercise a little or the day, at night, for advice!

Exercise 2: good listening skills

- Identify a topic that has caused tension lately. Let your spouse speak to describe how he or she experienced the situation.
- Listen carefully, and rephrase what he or she has just said.
- Ask him/her if you understood what he/she wanted to say.

- Now, imagine the scene from his or her point of view and experience the situation from his or her point of view. Try to feel what your partner may have been feeling at the time.
- Ask him/her how you could help him.
- Rephrase.
- Reverse the roles.

Exercise 3: express oneself in writing

Sometimes oral communication is not enough. You don't dare to confront a subject directly with your spouse, or you feel that the situation is blocked and that it will not be able to evolve. Maybe it's time to write a letter. Letters are not really fashionable anymore, it may seem outdated, and yet...

Writing has many benefits: it will liberate you, relieve you, and help you take a step back from the situation. Choose each word carefully and express yourself with kindness. This is not a settling of scores.

Describe what you feel, your needs, your desires, your hopes. Also tell him all the positive feelings you have for him. This is also the time to show your love if you find it difficult to express it to him on a daily basis.

Exercise 4: the reactions of the me!

In our relations with others, we always react according to 3 schemes described in Eric Berne's TA (Transactional Analysis). The Adult, the Child or the Parent. But what does this really reflect of us? What does it teach us about the way we act with others? Do we always behave in the same way, whatever the situation? Let's find out through this exercise.

Answer honestly to the 4 following questions, then find out the state of the Ego to which your answer corresponds.

1. You organize a painting workshop with your 7-year-old little cousin.

   a) Before you start, you decide together what you are going to paint and look for a model.
   b) You laugh when your little cousin thinks you are the canvas and you do the same with her.
   c) You establish strict rules: you must wear a smock to avoid getting dirty, and you are not allowed to put paint anywhere else than on the canvas.

2. You are training at the gym and the manager informs you that you have to interrupt your session because it is closing time.

   a) You look at the counter on your treadmill and calculate the total number of calories you've just burned.

- b) You hurry to stop the machine and gather your things to leave; it's already late and he must surely be tired from his day. So much for your shower, you'll take it at home.
- c) You turn off the machine you are on and go meekly to the changing rooms.

3. Your sister tells you she's pregnant with her first child.

- a) Immediately you are concerned about her condition and ask her if she is suffering from morning sickness.
- b) You jump for joy and shout that you are going to be the best uncle/auntie.
- c) You ask her how many weeks of amenorrhea she has.

4. You are a passenger on a motorcycle and the driver exceeds the speed limit and does not, in your opinion, drive safely.

- a) You clearly signal the driver to stop, get off the motorcycle and lecture the driver on how to ride.
- b) You make a clacking sound with your tongue in protest, which cannot be heard by the driver. When you reach your destination, you get off the motorcycle in a furious rage and leave without speaking to the driver.
- c) You say nothing and close your eyes so that you cannot see what is happening.

Correction and annotation:

Question 1:

1a. You behave like an adult, reasoning.

1b. Like a free child, you enjoy laughter and have fun.

1c. You are watching out for the grain! You teach him that there are rules to respect and that you must not do anything. This is the attitude of the normal parent.

Question 2:

2a. As an adult, you want to know if you have met your goals.

2b. This is an attitude that is consistent with that of a foster parent.

2c. When it's time, it's time. No arguing. This is similar to the reaction of a child who is adapted and submissive. Like when he followed what one of his parents asked him to do.

Question 3:

3a. Although you're happy for her, you're trying to find out how she's doing. You're acting like a foster parent to her child.

3b. You give free rein to your joy without restraint, as a free child would.

3c. Your rational side takes over and you wish to determine, with precision, the arrival of your niece or nephew. You act like an adult.

Question 4:

4a. Normative parent.

4b. You adopt the typical posture of the rebellious teenager. You express your dissatisfaction in a clearly visible way. This is called the rebellious Adapted Child.

4c. Submissive Adapted Child.

With this exercise you have been able to identify the behaviors you tend to adopt on a recurring basis.

None of these so-called "functional" behaviors are problematic; what is important is to be adaptable and to ensure that you maintain good communication, whether verbal or non-verbal. In everyday life, you will take turns adopting each of these states.

Exercise 5: my life position

In this exercise, we will try to find out what position you take in your daily relationships with others. Do you tend to be the leader? To follow the movement? Do you feel lost when you have to face things alone? Can you handle the pressure? Remarks?

What you think is just a detail actually reveals a lot about you.

For each point, check the answer that best defines you.

1. Do you find it hard to admit that you were wrong?

- Pretty much yes

- Pretty much no

2. Before making your final decision, do you manage to take into account the opinions of those around you, your impressions and the constraints?

- Pretty much yes

- Pretty much no

3. Do you still need to ask for validation to be sure?

- Pretty much yes

- Pretty much no

4. Do you tend to give your opinion easily?

- Pretty much yes

- Pretty much no

5. Do you feel the need for people to agree with you to keep doing what you do?

- Pretty much yes

- Pretty much no

6. Can you imagine people paying attention to you without you having to ask for it?

- Pretty much yes

- Pretty much no

7. Do you dare to ask others for help when you need it and in a direct way?

- Pretty much yes

- Pretty much no

8. Do you know, in the majority of cases, how to propose "win-win" solutions to resolve your conflict situations?

- Pretty much yes

- Pretty much no

9. Do you ever think you'd be better than the others?

- Pretty much yes

- Pretty much no

10. Do you tend to believe that you never do better than others?

- Pretty much yes

- Pretty much no

11. Do you have an objective view of your weaknesses and abilities?

- Pretty much yes

- Pretty much no

12. Do you like to take the lead when you're in a group?

- Pretty much yes

- Pretty much no

Comment:

If you answered "yes" to questions 3, 5, 6 and 10, it is because you have already experienced the role of the little "Calimero" several times. You sometimes feel injustice; you tend to devalue yourself and you are afraid of not pleasing others. You are in what is called the "OK- / OK+" position.

If you answered "yes" to questions 1, 4, 9 and 12, you are in the opposite position. You tend rather to never doubt yourself, to the point that you can be extremely dirigiste, even tyrannical with your entourage. This can even sometimes be seen as arrogance or self-sufficiency. In this pattern, you are more on the side of the persecutors than on the side of the victims. You are in what is called the "OK+ / OK-" position.

If you answered "yes" to questions 2, 7, 8 and 11, then you are at the balance point between listening to others and trusting yourself. You are aware of your strengths but also of your weaknesses and are not afraid to ask for help when necessary. You seek what is best for everyone, even if it means making compromises. You are in a position that is called "OK+ / OK+".

As you may have guessed, there is also a final position: the "OK- / OK-" position. Generally, this position corresponds to a phase where you find no quality, no added value, but not only. We also believe that everything around us is worthless and useless. This is usually a period of severe depression.

Don't worry, it is quite normal for you to have, once in your life, experienced one or other of these positions, and even all four. The main thing is to make sure you spend as much time as possible in the "OK+ / OK+" position.

Exercise 6: Identify A Drama Triangle

Throughout your life, and on many occasions, you will witness psychological games, especially that of the drama triangle. Regularly practice observing and identifying these situations, whether on the street, on vacation, or in the office... Because the more you pay attention to them, the easier it will be for you to avoid this infernal trap of the drama triangle, or even to avoid it, purely and simply.

Below is a fact that you have experienced or observed that seemed characteristic of each of these roles.

1. A situation experienced with a victim:

The experience: ....

Who? ....

How was it characteristic of this role:

....

....

2. A situation experienced with a persecutor:

The experience: ....

Who? ....

How was it characteristic of this role?

....

....

3. A situation experienced with a rescuer:

The experience: ....

Who? ....

How was it characteristic of this role:

....

....

Comment:

You may have seen it for yourself, but when you get into what is called the drama triangle, you may experience all three positions in turn. It's a bit like the game of musical chairs, and that's where the importance of identifying behaviors and getting around that triangle comes in.

Improve Intimacy with Your Partner

This is an area in which many couples experience difficulties, so I will include lots of links to further information and other resources in the back of this, but I also want to make a few broad points (some of which apply mainly to heterosexual couples).

For most women and some men, the desire to have sex in a relationship is, in my experience, completely dependent on how they feel about their partner in general.

In other words, making your partner feel loved, cared for, and supported, goes a long way towards sorting out any difficulties in this area.16

This is particularly so when the difficulty is that a partner who was once enthusiastic about sex, now appears to have lost all interest in it.

If your partner is feeling resentful towards you because you're not listening when they want to talk to you about things that are important to them (but may not be important to you), they are not going to look kindly at overtures towards sex that day, or anytime soon.

In unhappy relationships, at least one partner—often both—is feeling completely unloved, neglected and, because of this, resentful.

Ultimately, their needs in the relationship are not met. For a relationship to work long-term, both partners need to have their needs met in a balanced way.

If your partner has been feeling neglected, unloved, and resentful for years—as many partners in unhappy relationships have—the relationship will be close to breakdown.

In this scenario, it is unlikely that you will still be enjoying regular sex together.

Indeed, in this situation, it is more likely that sex has become just another chore, another demand, for at least one partner and often, this has been the case for years.

Often, one partner—usually, but not always, the woman—will complain about a lack of emotional connection and romance.

Of course, romance can mean many different things to different people. One useful question to ask yourself is, "What did my partner enjoy in the past?"

Sometimes, in this situation, affection will feel difficult. To the partner who is feeling unloved and neglected, a gesture of affection may be suspected to be just a tool being used as a lead-in to sex.

This can make a partner feel used and even more resentful.

Romantic gestures such as flowers or a candlelit meal can also be devalued in this way, however good the intention. If it feels to one partner that these things are only ever part of a request for sex, they will lose interest.

This is unfortunately common and ultimately counterproductive as it increases bad feelings and distrust.

If you are the partner who is always hoping for more sexual intimacy, try to be affectionate at other times without it always having to be about sex.

In these circumstances, it can be helpful to break the pattern by refraining from attempts to initiate sex —say for a month or six weeks — and to instead focus on bringing back the romance (see Case Study 2).

Also, remember the other two behaviors that heal and make them part of your daily life:

1. Attention and
2. Focus on the positive

I've seen many people who have done this.

After many weeks of feeling that they were getting nowhere they suddenly report that they have turned the corner and are back on track; back to cuddling, sleeping together, having days out with the kids, and having fun together in all its forms.

Often, all it takes is for at least one of you to "keep on keeping on"—as the song has it—because what goes wrong between people is a dynamic. If one person changes, the whole relationship can change.

However, be warned that you will need perseverance and determination to keep this up—day after day, week after week—often with nothing to show for it for a long time. So, think of it as a marathon rather than a sprint!

It can also be helpful to think of it as "winning your partner back"—a period of courtship to show them how much you love and value them (remember they are probably feeling neglected and hurt).

More problems with sex

Women were traditionally the gatekeepers for sex, as before reliable DNA tests, the only guarantee of paternity was the faithfulness of the woman.

In many cultures and time periods, women have been under huge pressure to be or appear to be asexual and chaste.

Even today, there are still very mixed messages in society about women's sexuality. In many cultures, sexuality and enjoyment of sex are seen as a good thing—in men and boys.

By contrast, virginity and chastity are still prized and even venerated, in women, in many religions and cultures. As a result, many people grew up believing that sex is something for men that is done to women.

There are still many insults available to shame women—but not men—who are sexually active. All these mixed, conflicting messages—not surprisingly—cause some women (and some men) problems in this area.

Women and girls often feel that they are expected to be sexy, but not sexual.18

In addition, whereas the most sexual part of a man's body (the penis) is clearly visible to them, and they are familiar with it and used to handling it from a young age, the most sexual part of a woman's body (the clitoris) is not necessarily familiar to her.

Also, because it has no function in reproduction (other than the pleasure of the woman) its importance has been overlooked in many cultures, until recently.

What women like sexually is not normally what we see in depictions of sex. Even today, male pleasure remains center stage.

Clitoral stimulation, which is central to most female's pleasure, still isn't usually shown in sex on screen, however otherwise explicit. It is also often not part of sex education despite its crucial role in sex for half the population.

Sex therapists say that enjoyment of sex is first learned through masturbation, but this is something that, for all these reasons, many women didn't do and don't feel comfortable with.

Because of all this, a woman may not have learned to enjoy her own body and may not be in touch with her own sexuality. These difficulties can be passed down from mother to daughter as well as through the wider culture; for example, through attitudes towards masturbation.

Like men, women must be aroused to enjoy sex. However, for all the reasons given above, many women have had even consensual sex, particularly when young, where they were not sufficiently aroused, and it was painful and unpleasant.

All of this, sadly, means that although women, in my experience, are as capable of enjoying sex as men, many women and girls have had only bad or frustrating experiences.

Times are changing—and thankfully, this is not the case for increasing numbers of women—but cultural practices and attitudes change slowly, so these things still affect many women and relationships today.

The Effects of Trauma

Another area of possible difficulty for both men and women is the effects of trauma. Experiences of sexual abuse and rape are unfortunately not uncommon and can leave survivors with long-lasting difficulties in many areas, often, especially in sexual relationships.

Human Givens Therapy has a specific evidence-based, intervention for trauma and other difficult experiences, which is very effective, in many cases, in relieving symptoms and distress. It does not involve re-living or talking in detail about what happened

Maintaining Your Relationship

Creating and maintaining relationships comes easy for partners that have a good relationship with each other.

When partners genuinely enjoy being in the same space, conversing, communing with each other and coexisting with each other, their relationship becomes effortless and smooth.

This also gives them a better understanding of each other's behavioral traits and quirks which helps them in predicting each other's behaviors, helps them to understand why one's partner behaves a certain way and guides them in acting accordingly.

Relationships with partners that are existing on the same wavelength and in total sync with each other are more likely to be long lasting and successful than relationships with partners that do not have a strong sense of relation between them.

Being in sync with one's partner aids effective communications as partners who are in sync with each other are able to understand both spoken and unspoken messages being passed across through body language.

When partners do not relate with other people properly, it is easy for partners to be oblivious to each other's sufferings and problems if they are not verbally shared.

This could cause an individual to feel lonely even in the relationship and become emotionally distant from his/her partner.

In order for partners to build emotional intimacy and reconnect their relationship, partners need to examine their level of relation with each other, and ask questions and have intimate enlightening conversations on how to deepen their relation with each other.

How Do We Relate With Each Other?

With the aim of building emotional intimacy and reconnecting relationships, partners have to find a means of relating better with each other. For partners to build intimacy there is a need for a sense of closeness and interdependence between them which can only be built when partners relate on a deeper level together.

To reach this level, partners need to ask questions about what drives them, where they feel the most safety, their history and experiences, and other factors that make him/her uniquely different from every other existing human being.

Every human has different vibes to them, different ways to get comfortable.

Some feel much relaxed and open only when they outdoors and one with mother nature's gifts.

Some people feel more of themselves when they listen to music and/or other forms of art.

It's just a matter of finding the 'it' for them.

You may find that they talk about that specific thing a lot, they like to be around it a lot, or it brings a certain level of peace, enthusiasm whenever they are around it.

Creating better relations with one's partner is a two-way street; both partners have to be willing to deepen the level of connection and communication between them to enhance a deeper level of intimacy and emotional connection between them.

Notwithstanding, there are certain gestures that go a long way in getting your partner to relate and connect better.

Using Positive and Motivation Words During Conversations.

When we use positive words on our partners and ultimately those around us, it tends to bring out their best sides, it makes them feel progressive and valuable. This can go a long way in ensuring a stable relationship. Even when faced with challenges from the workplace, societal pressure, it is really important that they believe there's someone who would always believe in them despite. As the saying goes "positive vibes, can only yield positive fruits".

- Endearing nicknames /pet names

Adults have found this to be very effective. Using nicknames for yourselves can help bring out the 'child-like' instincts in all of us. It makes them feel young again, playful, attractive, less tensed and special.

- Having shared memories and experiences

This involves planning and actually doing things together, going on vacations, planning special treats and dates for just you both, doing silly but less dangerous pranks on each other, video blogs, etc. owning something together gets the bonding hormones flowing.

- Respecting individuals' point of view and opinions

Whenever arguments arise, be it serious or not, it's always important to try to understand their side of the story. Trying to prove difficult will only give the impression that you are more apart and will hardly find common ground. This is really discouraging for any relationship even if the love started out strong. Ordinary arguments and disagreements can build up over time.

- Thoughtful gestures like giving surprising and unnecessary gifts

The act of gift giving has been the most effective way of showing your loved ones that they matter and that they are special.

It is really important not to underestimate the simple gesture of giving, more so, if it's a thoughtful gift, something they have always dreamt of having, something they love and even surprising those with newer packages can be a way of opening their hearts.

How Do You Keep Connected and In Sync With Each Other?

All relationships require efforts, commitment, and patience to stay alive and work.

It is easy to drift apart and lose the emotional connection between them when partners get too comfortable with each other and stop trying to keep the emotional connection intact.

In order for partners to stay emotional connection even when they are physically apart, there needs to be a level of trust and emotional security between partners that allows them to rest easy even when they are thousands of miles away from each other.

When partners have a complete sense of closeness, belonging and togetherness, it helps them feel secure in their emotional connection with each other, because then they know that no matter what happens, his/her is on the same team with them.

Different partners have different relationship dynamics. I.e.; what works for Mr. A in his relationship might not work for Mr. B in his own relationship.

This is a result of individual and behavioral differences.

Thus, different individuals in different relationships have different ways of staying in sync with his/her partner, based on their behaviors/personalities and the type of relationship they have.

Partners can be informed on how best to stay on sync with each other through asking questions and initiating intimate conversations. However, there are general universal tips that can be used to maintain sync between partners.

Here are some useful tips;

- Spend quality time with your partner

Planning and spending some time alone with your partner on a regular basis will help you both stay connected and feel special because quite often, as time goes, by we get entangled by work, raising a family and social duties and so we forget that it's important to keep the spark alive. You need yourselves of all the fun things you both did before all the extracurricular activities came into play.

Sitting face to face and in close proximity to your partner on a regular basis can help bring solace.

- Stay communicated

Whether short or long-distance relationships, all require adequate communications because communication makes your partner important, it keeps them updated on what you are going through at every point in time and it's very difficult to get back on track once the bridge in communication is broken and left unattended to.

This is the most vital part of every relationship. Make it a habit of telling your partner what you are going through and not making them guess. According to Lawrence Robinson, "if you have known each other for a while, you may assume that your partner has a pretty good idea of what you are thinking and what you need. However, your partner is not a mind reader. While your partner may have some idea, it is much healthier to express your needs directly to avoid any confusion.

- Give and take

Relationship is a give and take business. When you recognize what's important to your partner, it brings wholeness to him/her, it shows a measure of goodwill, thoughtfulness and a sense of devotion. Constantly giving to others at the expense of your own needs will only build resentment and anger

How deep is our emotional connection?

In romantic relationships, the level of emotional depth and dependency between both partners determines the strength of that relationship. Communicating with your partner does not guarantee that you do understand what he/she is going through and often, partners may feel like their significant other listens out of sense of duty, not because they genuinely care or feel the way they do which could lead to him/her feeling small and insignificant.

Emotional depth is being able to listen, interpret, and sensitively respond to feelings that arise in your partner, others around you and ultimately yourself.

This is the ability to show empathy, to 'feel into' someone else's experiences to know what it feels like to be them.

That level of interdependency gives both partners a sense of reliability, true friendship and a deep intimate connection that is built over time. This, as well as empathy takes time to become insoluble, because there are significant factors that affect the level of transparency and vulnerability needed between partners to achieve desired emotional depth and intimacy.

We often want our partner to be able to talk to us about everything and also to be the first person they think of sharing their emotions with whenever they going through something be it Positive or Negative but we also have to understand that no human being was ready made as certain factors such as early/childhood environmental factors, prominent life changing experience and events, gender and gender roles as dictated by society, and an individual's background and culture can affect and influence an individual's perception and personality which in turn dictates the individual's ability to understand, empathize and form emotional connections with his/her partner.

PART 2: Section I – Understanding Infidelity

Introduction

Confronting and speaking about infidelity within marriages has become an issue met with much taboo and hypocrisy. In today's society and the era in which we live, events of infidelity have become a much more likely phenomenon in many marital relationships. However, only a few couples will speak about this issue, much less to openly and honestly confront it. Within the dynamics of every sexually committed relationship, the possibility of infidelity is a real event that every couple must confront and address.

Ironically, infidelity has raised its ugly head in many social and structural settings. It has transcended the barriers of social-economic class, race, gender and even religion. It has made its entrance into homes, religious arenas, the white house, political campaign trails and organizations, and its effects in many marriages are undeniable.

For years, I have had a deep concern for marriages, seeing that I myself have been married for over fifteen (15) years. In my attempt to solidify my own marriage and give it the fighting chance that it so rightly deserves, I also had to confront the issue of 'Infidelity' and this concept of 'The Other Woman'. Hence, this is for a mature woman who is willing to lay aside the plethora of her emotional basket, to gain great wisdom and a deeper insight into the hooks, strategies and operations of 'The Other Woman'.

If as couples, we intend to sincerely live happy and fulfilling marriages, we must now be willing to closely examine the dynamics of 'infidelity'. Deeply embedded within this dynamic is a crucial and noteworthy element called 'The Other Woman'. For a lot of wives, this conversation regarding 'her' is often met with feelings of great offense and personal inadequacies. However, I believe that one of the key elements in confronting and addressing this issue is to closely examine the operations of 'this woman'. To investigate her hooks, strategies and to carefully examine the table she prepares and spreads for husbands.

Let me make this unequivocally clear, I am not glorifying the concept of this 'The Other Woman'. However, it is my sincere intention to empower, equip and duly inform every wife about the strategies, hooks and offerings of these side chicks. In so doing I intend to expose the secret weapons and empires created by these ladies. Neither am I suggesting that the actions or inactions of wives are the main reasons for infidelity or failed marriages. However, based on my research and discussions with men, I am suggesting that the ideas found in this, are noteworthy of every wife in examining this matter more closely. Even the good admonishes us by saying 'My people are destroyed for lack of knowledge' (Hosea 4: 6, King James Version) It further states that we should not let the enemy outsmart us because we are not ignorant of his devises (2 Corinthians 2:11, New Living Translation)

Finally, please note that the ideas and principles highlighted in this are not meant to be broad-brush advice for every wife. These strategies and ideologies are not guaranteed to stop any case of infidelity.

However, if as couples we intent to truly live healthy, happy and fulfilling marriages, then we must begin this discussion with our spouses. We must honestly examine 'the man in the mirror'. We must be honest enough to examine our weaknesses and strengths to fortify our marriages, making them stronger and better.

What is Infidelity?

To give meaning to "infidelity" using a single definition is quite challenging because its incidences vary from person to person. Usually, infidelity is also termed as "cheating" or "having an affair" with someone else. One is said to be practicing infidelity if he/she is not being completely faithful to his/her partner, but there are other ways to define infidelity:

Sexual attraction – This is one of the most common signs of infidelity. Sometimes, a person develops a sexual attraction towards another person even if he/she is committed to someone else whether they are married or simply dating. Infidelity occurs when a person develops a sexual desire towards another person and he/she acts on it instead of trying to overcome these wrong feelings.

Romantic emotional connection – A person is said to be cheating if he/she develops a romantic emotional connection with someone other than his/her current partner. This connection can manifest in different ways, whether through gestures or by feeling that the other person is someone he/she wants to be with.

Untruthfulness – Even without the sexual attraction and the romantic emotional connection with someone else, some people say that their partner is practicing infidelity if he/she is being dishonest with him/her. For example, they miss out on some important details when talking to their partner, but they reveal these removed details to another person. Another example could be seeing another person in secret or going out on dates without telling their partner about it. Simply lying to one's partner is a sign that something is wrong in their relationship; distrust is a sign of a dwindling relationship, most especially if you prefer to share your life experiences with other people than your partner.

Causes of Infidelity

When a person finds out that his/her partner is cheating on him/her, he/she may ask the following questions: "Why? Is there something wrong with me?" "Am I not good enough?" "What did I do wrong?" There is no complete list of answers to these questions as well as the causes of infidelity, but here are the most common ones, separated into the physical and emotional aspect, that may help you address your questions:

Emotional aspect

- **Incompatibility** – One of the main reasons why people cheat is because they are not getting along well with their current partner but they do not have the heart to break up because they think they can still "work things out". However, sometimes they don't work out and the person ends up looking for someone else to fulfill his emotional needs while forgetting that he/she is still committed to someone else.

- **Romantic emotional connection** – When a person meets someone else and they get along well, there is a possibility that they may develop a strong, romantic emotional connection without asking for it. In the process of getting to know each other, there is a possibility that one may feel like the other person is someone fun to be with and is someone who would make a good partner instead of the one he/she is currently with.

- **Weariness and boredom** – Another common reason why some people cheat is that they are already tired of the relationship in the sense that they are already getting bored. When someone feels like nothing exciting is happening anymore, he/she could go out and look for someone to provide him/her that lost "excitement".

Physical aspect

- **Sexual attraction** – When it comes to the physical aspect of infidelity, one of the most common causes of infidelity and broken relationships is a sexual attraction towards another person other than the current partner. We all have our desires and fantasies, but sometimes some people cannot suppress these desires even if they know well that they are still committed, which is why they end up cheating on their partner because they try to fulfill these desires.

- **Amount of time together** – Partners may not always have the same careers. They meet different people every day and spend most of their hours with different sets of people. However, when someone spends a lot of time with another person, there is a possibility that they will develop feelings for each other, most especially if their interests go along well and they do not allow themselves to be held back by last commitments.

- **Absence** – Spending too much time away of your partner can also cause too much longing, and most of the time this "longing" is the cause of infidelity, for there is a tendency for them to look for someone who would fill the "gaps" that their partner had left.

- **Long-distance** – It is difficult for long-distance relationships to prosper especially if one is not always updated on the activities of the other. Same as absence, long-distance relationships barely survive because of either one of the two looks for some excitement and romance without thinking of their partners. Oftentimes, they do this because they think they can never be caught because of the distance separating the two of them.

These are just some of the causes of infidelity, there are a whole lot more. However, what must be remembered is that caught or not caught, secret or not secret, infidelity is still cheating, and cheating is a big sin to commit to one's partner, and there cannot be a proper explanation for cheating because if only two people knew to trust and love each other, then there would be no need to look for someone else to do that job.

How to react when you find catch your partner in infidelity

The most obvious reaction anyone could have if they catch their partner cheating is shock and anger. A huge fight is expected to occur, as well as a lot of crying, blaming, and explanation. However, shouting at one another, not letting the other explain, and simply crying does not make a nice solution to dealing with infidelity. How does one properly react when they catch their partner cheating?

Try to keep calm

This piece of advice may seem mediocre to some of you, but it is one of the most important things that you must remember when dealing with a busted partner. This is important because you can think clearly if you have a calm mind. Most importantly, it will save both of you from the embarrassment of causing a scene if you are able to regain your composure even after discovering a drastic thing.

Confront your partner

Confronting your partner does not mean entering his/her room, throwing things around, and shouting at him/her asking him/her who the other person is. Confronting your partner means trying to get honest answers from him/her. Confrontation must be done in perfect timing, most importantly if the two of you are alone. Confronting your partner with shouting, kicking, and other violent means will just make him/her fight back and thus keep the two of you from talking about things, which is why it is important for you to confront your partner calmly.

Do not let anger cloud your judgment

It is natural for you to get angry if you catch your partner cheating, who wouldn't be? However, if you really want to fix things, then you must listen and try to understand what your partner has to say. Allowing your anger to cloud your judgment and keep you from comprehending your partner's words will not do you any good, for being narrow-minded will not fix your relationship.

Allow your partner to explain

One of the things that you would want to know once you catch your partner cheating is the reason why. However, remember that you will not understand why if you will not let your partner explain in the first place. Even though it is a big mistake to do, your partner still has the right to explain. The beauty of listening to other people's explanations is that you will be able to weigh your decisions more carefully according to his/her explanations, and you might also pick up important life lessons along the way. For example, your partner cheated on you because there is something wrong with your attitude and he can't stand it, he'd rather look for someone else. Listening to this kind of explanation may hurt, but in the end, it will tell you what went wrong and it will make you realize what you can do to make it right.

Coping with Infidelity

If you and your partner come to a mutual agreement that despite the affair that one of you has had, you wish to save the marriage. You need to agree that your relationship pre-affair was a valuable one and you think that it is worth fighting for. Once you come to this agreement, there are several things that you will need to consider and carry out.

1. The first thing that needs to be done (obviously) is for the affair to end. It is not possible for a relationship to work if a third party is involved. There should be no casual meetings occurring with that person in case there is a danger of a lapse. If the person was an office colleague, you might be wise to even change jobs.

2. It is not going to be an easy task to get back together again and rebuild. So be warned that there will be some turmoil, some ups and downs. You need to ride through this calmly and not get spooked at the first down that occurs.

3. If you are the one who has had the affair and your partner wants to discuss it, you need to do it in an open and honest manner. No half-truths or evasive replies are going to help at this point. In fact, it would be very detrimental to your relationship at this juncture if you are not completely honest.

4. You also need to be accountable to your partner now. It is natural for your partner to have trust issues. If your partner needs constant reassurance and needs to know your whereabouts all the time, then

you need to provide it. Expecting trust to kick in at once is not reasonable.

5. You need to make an honest promise that this will not be repeated again. And if your partner needs to hear this several times, it needs to be said.

6. The path forward has to be decided by the person betrayed. If he/she (the one betrayed) needs time, it has to be provided and the person who has had the affair needs to be extra understanding and considerate.

7. The partner who had the affair needs to introspect on why this affair occurred. What caused him/her to stray? There could be things that need to be changed in order for it not to reoccur.

8. Moving forward is the responsibility of both partners. The onus cannot lie on just one. Both need to put in the effort and work at their marriage to make it a success.

9. Above all be patient with yourself and each other. Spend time nurturing each other and your relationship.

Heal from Infidelity

We tend to be naive, before our trust is broken by someone we care about. Maybe that moment hit us in grade school, when we found out a close friend was something else when we were out of earshot. Or maybe this is our first real relationship, and discovering the pain of betrayal came with it.

Either way, we tend to go into relationships with a certain crust of naiveté. Whether we've been hurt before to this extent or not, we carry the implicit belief that this new relationship is the start of something new and beautiful, that there is a solid chance that it will all work out and we will push through anything that gets in our way.

Maybe, just maybe, the naiveté has exclusively to do with this particular form of betrayal. We thought that no matter what else happens to us, whatever fights we got into with each other, there was always an implicit promise that we would always be a team.

And now, maybe, we're not.

That stings. We've come this far with our partners, through the foundations we laid in the beginning, the relationship we worked hard to build, the discovery of their infidelity, and the discussions following it, but it still stings, because now a certain question hangs in the air:

Can I trust you again?

In the aftermath of their infidelity, there is a certain inability to trust our partner. They've lied, manipulated and covered up their deceptions and made a fool of us. Trust is one of the basic building blocks of a relationship and the commitment we made each other was based on trust. On a promise and a pledge. When that trust is broken, the relationship's foundation cracks. Without trust, the rest of the relationship starts heading towards a slow disintegration.

So, the question is untestable. We have to ask ourselves: Can I trust you again?

For those who conclude the answer is no, there is a relatively simpler path to follow. We need to decide whether their betrayal only extends to a relationship, or whether we now have to be concerned about every venture we've done together and where else we cannot trust them. It's not easy, but it's simple enough.

If the relationship is the only avenue where we feel trust issues would continue, then the relationship may be the only thing that has to fail. We don't need to block them across all our social media, we don't need to tell our friends to be careful dealing with our ex-partner, and so on and so forth. We can grow back into being friends, and no more, no less. If that is indeed what we want.

Of course, if the reverse is true, do that by all means. We may have to extricate ourselves from their lives as much as humanly possible. We need to cut them out like they're a cancerous tumor – which they may just be. Just remember that we're ultimately doing it for ourselves, and trying not to hurt anyone that doesn't have to be in the process. If our partner doesn't want to accept that, tough. They made the error when they cheated on us. This is just how we decided it should play out.

However, what happens when we have that voice in our heads that says Give them another chance?

Do we? Should we? Well, yes. But, again, only if we really want to. And only if we're reasonably sure that the second chance we're giving them won't be wasted.

See, we entered this relationship with a certain degree of naiveté, and that's perfectly fine, but that illusion has just been broken. For all intents and purposes, our partner is now on probation, and we're the no-nonsense parole officer. We accept no excuses, we take no sass, and we rule with a (reasonable) iron fist.

Our partner may feel that it's unfair of us to ask them not to meet their female friends and/or colleagues alone again, but we must keep in mind that the line has already been crossed. They must keep in mind that they've already crossed that line. We're not being paranoid, we're not being overly restrictive, we're advising them of what makes us comfortable and what they need to do to keep us that way in the light of their offenses. They must be willing to faithfully follow up on what they agreed to do— or not do. If they can't do that, this may not be a relationship worth salvaging. There should be zero tolerance for slip-ups now.

Trust is earned. And trust takes time, especially after that thin veneer of naiveté has been pulled aside.

We already went through the motions of meeting a stranger, or being introduced to them, or running into them with our shopping cart at the mall, or having your friend hit them with your van, what have you. The meet-cute is long past and, in the time since then, we put some effort into letting them into our lives and into our hearts. That's already been done.

What comes it then follows, will likely be more difficult, but this is absolutely normal. In fact, we're entitled to take as much time as we want to allow our partner back into our innermost self, that place where we feel safe allowing them certain liberties without suspicion or judgment. It is possible to arrive at this point, past our humiliation and our hurt and our anger, to be able to trust our partner again. We all make mistakes. Human beings are not infallible. But we can also learn from our mistakes, so as to avoid repeating them.

That said, there is also no reason that we should push ourselves to get all the way to that point again. Let's say that we were 99% percent confident in our partner's faithfulness prior to the recent revelation. We had near complete faith in them, there is no need for us to get to 99% with them ever again. They might desire it of us, they may even be completely worthy of it, but they no longer have the right to ask, and they should understand this.

The preferred outcome will probably be the best compromise the two of us can make. Maybe enough time passes and they earn back 75% of our trust. Enough to go shopping alone, but not enough to spend the night over at a friend's house. Enough to work an extra hour or two, but not enough to work late nights. Wherever we feel most comfortable drawing the line is exactly where we should draw it.

That's not to say that we must pull this idea to its extremes. Any compromise takes two people to participate, and even though it's on our partner to accept our terms, the terms still have to be reasonable. We can't demand they never see their friends again, or hold them hostage from living a life apart from us entirely. Remember what the topic earlier, that is also one surefire way to sabotage the relationship on its own: enforced togetherness.

Both of us have to want to be with each other, or it won't work.

It may help to talk it over with close friends or family, but let's be careful not to pay attention to the more exuberant members of our social circle. Saner minds prevail, and we should be careful that our advisers too are worth the time we ask of them. With that warning in mind, we should seek people who aren't afraid to help us draw the line, and help us walk through what we should and should not do.

For example:

Do offer praise or positive feedback if our partner takes it upon themselves to stay out of situations, we'd be uncomfortable with, without being asked. That's good.

Do not set fire to their cat if they forget to kiss us goodbye before they leave for work. That's very bad.

Of course, all of this is in service of the hope that we can eventually fix what has been broken. That may not be the case, however, we may see sign after sign that it's not going well.

They aren't talking to us, they aren't willing to take responsibility, they aren't putting in any sort of work on the relationship, they are easily given to argument, they shoot down all our ideas and offer none of their own, and so on. The list of red flags is long and expansive. So, what do we do?

We repeat our mantra. We stop, we breathe, we think.

Men and Women: Differences

Differing Responses of Men and Women to Infidelity

I will begin with a few statistics about men and women regarding infidelity and its consequences.

Men are usually considered to cheat more, but is that true? New research has revealed surprising facts about infidelity. Recent statistics show that more than one-half of men cheat on their partners, exactly 57 percent. But women are not far behind, 54 percent admit to infidelity.

Interestingly, they are more likely to seek a divorce than men. About 71 percent of divorces are initiated by women. Also, 53 percent of marriages end in divorce. Otherwise, 69 percent of women admitted they had chosen to be unfaithful because they no longer received any gifts from their partner, precisely of the kind of attention that makes women feel valued, and loved.

Cheating results in a loss of trust, and it is not a behavior that is unique to only one sex. Both men and women cheat. At this time, we will focus on the woman's perspective, but that does not mean that men cannot learn something valuable by reading this. If I tell you this story from the perspective of both men and women, you will not understand this well. Instead, we will focus on one gender, so that you will understand this better.

Read this carefully

There is a big difference in understanding cheating and the actual definition of infidelity, and it seems that different people come to different conclusions on the subject. For some, infidelity is the physical act of engaging in sexual relations with other people. Anything short of that does not count as cheating, at least not for them. Other people consider that infidelity is romantic physical contact, which should only be reserved for a partner, even if it does not include sexual intercourse.

There is more than one truth

Some believe that infidelity can exist even if there is no physical contact. If two people have shared something personal and intimate that would ordinarily be reserved only for a partner that is also infidelity.

The fact is, if your partner is convinced that you have cheated, because of the time, attention, or attachment you have given to another person, then you have committed infidelity. Your relationship should be the most important thing in the world to you and yes, friendships are wonderful, but if they impair intimacy and connection with your partner, then you are guilty of infidelity. That is a simple fact.

But what about when you are the "other woman"?

Relationships should be built on trust and mutual respect. When you are the "other woman" how can you trust a person who cheats on your partner with you? If he cheats with you, do you have enough ego and vanity to believe that he won't cheat on you too?

Now will you realize…

One thing psychologists know about cheating that the public ignores is that cheating never happens because of the quality of the relationship you are in. It is not because she was not good enough. Cheating happens because something is wrong with the person who is cheating.

Morality

There is no excuse that justifies infidelity. If the relationship is in trouble, then work on the problems. I have told you this so many times and I will continue to do so, because it is a very important thing for you to understand.

Crucial things

If you find that the relationship cannot be rescued, then break it, with divorce if you are married, or by leaving your partner if it's a relationship. Do this before you go looking for someone else. Don't cheat! Cheating can never be justified and is never acceptable.

There is even worse

One thing as bad as cheating is being the enabler of the cheater. Of course, that doesn't hold true if the person doesn't know that their lover is in a relationship with someone. In such a case, the man should take full responsibility and consequences for his actions.

But if the other person is aware of the situation, and chooses to continue the affair with the married man, then she is no better. It might be said that this other woman's infidelity is more unforgivable than his, because, as a woman, she should understand how much infidelity hurts and should never have entered into an affair.

As you look at the facts, bearing in mind that the problem of infidelity is not in the relationship, but in the one who committed the infidelity, then you will understand that the other woman can never be sure that she will not be deceived as well.

Golden rule

Once a cheater, always a cheater. If he is cheating, let him seek help. If it cheats again, you should just leave. But what do you do when you're with a cheater and you know he's cheated on other women before you? The truth is, a man who has a past of cheating cannot be trusted in a relationship.

And if you are the "other woman" ask yourself this question: Knowing his unfaithful history, what do you think it will be like to become the cheated one, and learn that he has moved on to another?

Learn the truth

Of course, you will think that things will be different with you. You will be everything he needs, but you are wrong. Again, it's not about the relationship, it's about the person cheating. Something deep in that person is broken, and sometimes just can't be fixed.

It's not in our power

There is nothing you can do, or give, or become, that will prevent a cheater from embarking on his "ventures". Cheating is cheating, both emotionally and physically, and if you allow it to continue, you are as guilty as he is. Don't worry, the time will come when, one day, he decides to move on to someone else, leaving you heartbroken just like the heart you helped him break when you participated in and encouraged his infidelity.

The Worst Thing that a Man does to Woman: Leaving her Alone but Married

Not all men are cheats. Some are truly loving, willing to give anything for their partner, and be loyal to the end. This is the type of man you need to look for, instead of constantly trying to fix an irreparable cheat that will only break your heart and the hearts of other women.

If your man comes directly from the arms of another woman, you should flee, because it will soon be your turn. If you don't, well, you've earned you everything it will do to your heart and your soul. Cheaters never win. Be honest with your partner, and if you prefer to be with someone else, then end the relationship immediately. If, you are the "other woman," you must also end the affair immediately. That is the right thing to do, or one day you will be in the place of this devil's wife, but, unlike his ex-partner, you will deserve every second of suffering.

This was written for cheaters. Infidelity is a major social issue and I will not clarify or classify specific reasons. Do you wonder why? Because of that "golden rule". I have criticized the cheaters and I believe that you understand why. I can give you false excuses for both men and women, but I would be lying to you. The truth is that there are no scruples in the cheater and they do things the wrong way. Both men and women are the same. And, there are no excuses.

Section II – Healing from Infidelity

The First Phase: The Crisis Phase

One of the main problems arising from couple's therapy is that it is viewed by many people as a last resort. It is often seen as something that partners turn to when they are unable to resolve conflicts on their own or have gone through a major relationship-affecting event such as infidelity.

Thanks to this view, most couples come to therapy too late. Many couples seek help when their relationship difficulties are already significantly entrenched. Research indicates that most couples have struggled for an average of six years before they finally decide to seek outside help. At this point in time, damaging behavior has already been entrenched and the bonds between the partners have been significantly weakened. There may also be a high level of resentment as a result of past hurts and disagreements.

This is not to say, however, that couples with deeply entrenched issues cannot work through them. But the earlier couples embrace treatment, the easier it will be to unravel the damaging behavior that has led to each issue.

Another problem arises when partners see couples' therapy as their chance to "change" their partner. This difficulty often rears its head when one party enters treatment believing they are in the right and their partner is the problem. For therapy to be effective, it is crucial for both partners to openly examine their behavior and be open to making the necessary changes. Beginning a therapy session with pre-conceived notions of who is right and wrong can hinder the process and deepen the rift between you and your partner. Instead of placing blame at your partner's feet, be open to the possibility that you are both able to make changes to better the relationship as a whole.

The tasks of the betrayed	➢ Expect a mixture of emotions
	➢ Take care of yourself
	➢ Don't wallow in self pity
	➢ Talk to a couple's counselor
The tasks of unfaithful	➢ Take responsibility for behavior
	➢ Reflect on your behavior
	➢ Give your partner space
	➢ Understand your partner's feelings
	➢ Keep your promises

Questions, Solutions, Exercises	➢ Is your partner willing to live transparency from now on? ➢ Do you feel your partner is genuinely remorseful? ➢ Is your partner willing to get help with dealing with the underlying issues that lead them to making the choices they did?

Each and every one of us who embarks on a romantic relationship will likely face one or more of the problems. It is human nature to disagree, and when we spend our lives so closely attached to another person, it is inevitable that conflict will arise.

But it is my hope that this has shown you the way forward – shown you that, however damaged your relationship, it can be fixed.

As you have no doubt recognized, many of the solutions presented here revolve around one key element: open and honest communication. This is the essence of resolving all conflict, whether with your spouse, or anyone else in your life.

When we are open and honest, we are creating a space for effective communication; communication that can get to the heart of any issue — and then begin to resolve it.

So, as you go forth and begin to mend the cracks in your relationship, focus on how you can keep the channels of communication with your loved one as open as possible. It will not always be easy — but it will be worth it.

The Second Phase: The Role of Grief

Grief and Loss

Human beings face loss on a daily basis. We may hardly notice the smaller ones. They do not hurt so much. But the larger, more emotional losses take time to heal. Grief is a normal response to the trauma of loss, just as a wound or burn is to physical trauma.

Many of our clients have found it helpful to understand and discuss the five stages of grief identified by Dr. Elisabeth Kübler Ross. We hope that you will be reassured to know that the raw emotions and the ups-and-downs that you may be suffering have also been experienced by others. However, not everyone goes through all five stages. In fact, they are not necessarily sequential, and sometimes people jump back and forth among them on their way to recovery.

Stage 1: Denial

"This can't be happening to me. I must be dreaming." If you have thoughts like this, you may be experiencing denial, the first stage. It is similar to the reactions of people who have experienced other losses, including death. Your initial reaction to the discovery that your mate has been unfaithful may be disbelief. In physical injury, shock is the body's way of protecting you against the reality of hurt in case the pain becomes too great to bear. Just as the body grows numb, so can the human heart. The numbness may last for a short or long time, depending on how long you need protection against your emotional pain. You may recognize denial in your situation, or if not, you may have seen it in operation with someone you know.

Many believed that Hillary Clinton was in a state of denial in the early stages of the president's relationship with Monica Lewinsky. But reality set in when she was confronted with fact after fact and finally with the stained blue dress. Kenneth Starr's summons to testify must have been a severe blow to her denial.

We must remember that denial is not purposeful, but an unconscious process that protects us from unbearable pain.

Stage 2: Anger

After denial, the offended spouse is likely to experience an explosive outpouring of anger. If you are feeling rage, you can be assured it is an expected response to discovering infidelity. At this stage some people scream and cry, and others vow revenge. The urge to retaliate may be very strong. It is at this stage that we see the woman who tosses her husband's clothes outside the house or gives his best Armani suits to the Goodwill. One woman reported that after her husband found out about her affair, he smashed her teapot collection.

One of our clients, Barbara, whose husband had been unfaithful to her, expressed her feelings at this stage by exclaiming, "I'm absolutely furious. To think he would have the nerve to carry on that way right under my nose. The louse! I could kill him." She sobbed, "After the pain he's caused me, I want him to suffer too."

When you are able to acknowledge your anger and express it in a safe way, you are on your way to working through your grief. We will discuss this stage in more depth and provide you with some tools to handle this powerful emotion.

Stage 3: Bargaining

When the anger dissipates, the bargaining stage begins. Beginning to face the fact that your marriage is in a crisis, you may start bargaining. "I promise to be more considerate." "I'll be more loving." "I'll try to be better in bed." "I'll change my ways and be more attentive." In the bargaining stage, you may be so hurt and terrified of losing the relationship that you are not able to think rationally.

Betty Jean, a faithful member of our support group on infidelity, told us how she wanted to impress her husband with her devotion, and she did so by ironing his shirts when he went on dates. Members of the group were angry with her. They correctly saw this behavior as supporting his infidelity and not standing up for herself. Betty Jean replied to their challenge by saying that he soon would realize what a fine wife and capable person she was to rise above the situation. Her husband left anyway.

Harvey told a similar story in his support group. Harvey was a criminal lawyer who relied on his logical skills to prepare his cases. Yet he told the group that he stayed home with the kids so that his wife could go to the theater and ballet with her lover. He went along with his wife's belief that she needed to get more out of life, since she was so young when they married. He reasoned that she would soon see who the better man was. But Harvey was mistaken; she didn't.

Stage 4: Depression

The fourth stage is depression. Tears may flow. You may feel lethargic and lose interest in the outside world. Your appetite may dwindle, or you may find yourself eating uncontrollably. Concentration may be difficult. You may become forgetful or confused.

"I was so depressed, I couldn't seem to get going," recalled one of our clients who was reacting to her husband's affair. "At first I only went through the motions, doing what I absolutely had to. I was frozen, immobilized." Another client said, "I know it's foolish to cry so much, but I can't stop. Nothing seems worth living for anymore."

Once you are depressed you may actually become your own worst enemy. For example, Princess Diana expressed her pain over her husband's infidelity through her suicide attempts, bulimia, and her extramarital affairs. Instead of caring for yourself, you may neglect yourself or your appearance. Instead of seeking pleasure, you may actually avoid it. We have heard our clients say things like, "If only I'd been more sexually responsive, he might not have strayed." "How could I have been such a blind fool?" You may falsely believe that you're being punished or that you actually deserve what happened. If you are experiencing similar thoughts or physical symptoms such as sleeplessness, loss of appetite, or inability to concentrate, medication prescribed by a psychiatrist may minimize your suffering and enable you to recover more quickly.

After discovering the affair, you can expect to experience sad feelings as important anniversary dates approach. Many women have come to our office concerned about the sadness they were feeling when they had felt they were moving forward and making progress in their recovery. In talking with them, we often found that this sadness was due to the approach of a birthday, a wedding anniversary, or the date of the discovery of the affair.

So, if you feel what you think is unexplained sadness, it is possible that there is a significant anniversary approaching. This in itself helps you, because understanding the cause of your feelings is often therapeutic. However, you can often do more for yourself by planning activities you enjoy and rallying your support system to your aid.

Stage 5: Acceptance

The final stage, acceptance, is necessary for moving forward. There are two kinds of acceptance: intellectual, which comes earlier, and emotional, which comes. Intellectual acceptance means understanding what has happened. Emotional acceptance means being able to discuss your spouse's infidelity without the intense reaction you experienced earlier.

You must remember that acceptance is the final stage of grieving. If you are at the earlier stages, this last stage may seem like an impossibility. We have heard many clients say, "I can never accept what happened." Condoning infidelity is not the same as acceptance. Acceptance simply means you have acknowledged that infidelity has occurred. The consequences for non-acceptance are bitterness and an inability to trust again. In our experience, after enough time passes, most people are able to integrate both the emotional and intellectual acceptance of their loss.

If you have only recently discovered that your spouse has been unfaithful, understanding the stages of grief and loss will not alone be enough to end your suffering. You should be aware that the grief process may vary in time with different people, from a very short duration to a very protracted length of time. As much as infidelity seems like a death, it is a death of the hopes you had had when you were first married. It is not necessarily the death of the marriage itself. You may be able to rebuild and create new dreams.

The Third Phase: Understanding

Before choosing to end the relationship or go on with it, there are some questions you need to consider.

- Are there things in the relationship worth fighting for now?
- Is there another chance of love and reconnection?
- If we go on, will we have a real relationship or is this just a convenient way of meeting our shared goals?
- Is it love or will we be together for the sake of the children and other mutual interests?

Sometimes, the rift arising between two people after a case of infidelity is so vast that it cannot be put together. If that is the case, accept it and decide openly and with courage and love to fight or not fight for the relationship knowing that it will be challenging. There is nothing as tiresome as fighting to hold on to someone or something that is not interested. If it is the case, be honest and save your energy. A relationship where someone has deep and important needs that are not being met will not be sustainable.

If you are the one who had an affair, it is now time to guard your relationship and make boundaries. As with any traumatizing experience, finding out about an affair will generate a massive potential for re-experiencing the shocks over and over. Here is how: every time there is a gap or some form of unexplained event in your relationship, panic will set in. Any unanswered calls, missed texts, the phone off, getting a voice message, your location unknown, and you have not reported, your spouse will feel insecure. Any time you are not

where you said you would be, you are home late without an explanation, you did not keep a promise you made, and any other thing that is associated with a continuing affair will make you answerable. There will be recurring feelings of betrayal, panic, anger, fear, sadness, loneliness, suspicion, loss, among others. The shocks of trauma will keep recurring, and they should not be hurried. Let everyone take their time to heal.

Be accountable every minute of the day. Stay open, and let there be no secrets. Knowing that you are honest and open will help the heart heal from trauma and anxiety that comes from discovering the affair. Your cheated-on spouse will look for information even though there is nothing to find out. The porpoise of looking is not to find but to make sure that there is nothing in secret. For wholesome healing to happen, it will be your turn to be responsible and stand in the guard of your relationship boundaries for a while.

Be accountable to the extent that there are no gaps, no missing pieces, and no absences in the day. There should be no secrets. If the person you cheated with contacts you, make sure that you report to your partner before he/she even gets suspicious. Be on the frontline to make things safe again. For the betrayed person, there will be the need to find reassurance and evidence that the affair is not taking place anymore. This need might last for years, and it might even appear like an obsession. Finding out about a case of infidelity is very traumatizing, and the only way a betrayed person will recover is by searching for proof that the partner is truthful and the relationship is safe.

Acceptance	• Try another option • Move on
The tasks of the betrayed	• Forgive yourself first: for feeling angry, for feeling sad, for doubting yourself. Forgive yourself for being hateful and even contemplating revenge. Forgive yourself for not realizing that things are wrong in the relationship. Forgive yourself for not taking the right steps as soon as you noticed something was wrong. Let go of the feeling of self-doubt, shame, mistrust. Forgive yourself for wanting to leave and wanting to stay. Forgive yourself for the feelings you felt before the affair and after. • Every relationship has its ups and downs. There is a make it or break it point for every two people in a commitment. Some relationships

will have one weak point while others will have limitless. Your relationship involved two people, and if your partner felt unfulfilled, it was up to him/her to tell you and ask for support. If he/she asked and you were not attentive, then forgive yourself and take the lesson. There might have been times when your needs went unfulfilled too, but you did not choose to stray. These unfulfilled moments will happen in every relationship once in a while. It is the duration and intensity that marks the difference in damage. The longer a person has to wait, the higher the chances for cheating. You deserve the opportunity to know when things are not right; therefore, find a cure. You deserve the chance to repair the developing holes. You are getting it now as you work on your healing. Forgive yourself if you do not have the chance to give your partner what he/she needs henceforth.

	Sometimes, a great relationship will not occur even if you offer all you have. Sometimes, the relationship will not fail just because one person is broken; rather, it is the combination of the two people.
The tasks of the unfaithful	- If you are the one who had an affair, it is now time to guard your relationship and make boundaries. As with any traumatizing experience, finding out about an affair will generate a massive potential for re-experiencing the shocks over and over. Here is how: every time there is a gap or some form of unexplained event in your relationship, panic will set in. Any unanswered calls, missed texts, the phone off, getting a voice message, your location unknown, and you have not reported, your spouse will feel insecure. Any time you are not where you said you would be, you are home late without an explanation, you did not keep a promise you made, and any other

thing that is associated with a continuing affair will make you answerable. There will be recurring feelings of betrayal, panic, anger, fear, sadness, loneliness, suspicion, loss, among others. The shocks of trauma will keep recurring, and they should not be hurried. Let everyone take their time to heal.

- Be accountable every minute of the day. Stay open, and let there be no secrets. Knowing that you are honest and open will help the heart heal from trauma and anxiety that comes from discovering the affair. Your cheated-on spouse will look for information even though there is nothing to find out. The porpoise of looking is not to find but to make sure that there is nothing in secret. For wholesome healing to happen, it will be your turn to be responsible and stand in the guard of your relationship boundaries for a while.

	• Be accountable to the extent that there are no gaps, no missing pieces, and no absences in the day. There should be no secrets. If the person you cheated with contacts you, make sure that you report to your partner before he/she even gets suspicious. Be on the frontline to make things safe again. For the betrayed person, there will be the need to find reassurance and evidence that the affair is not taking place anymore. This need might last for years, and it might even appear like an obsession. Finding out about a case of infidelity is very traumatizing, and the only way a betrayed person will recover is by searching for proof that the partner is truthful and the relationship is safe.
Questions, Solutions, Exercises	• How do you feel about your spouse compared to the other person you had an affair?

- What do you miss about your spouse and the other person?
- How do you feel about your spouse?
- Do you still miss your spouse?
- Does his infidelity make you feel like you will never be able to have a valid relationship?
- Are you still afraid of losing your spouse? Do you think you are still worthy of his/her love?
- What is it about me that your spouse still wants?
- Which part of your relationship is worth fighting for now?
- What do you still want in your relationship?
- Can the rage, anger, and devastation we feel now change to positive feelings?

Acceptance – Love Yourself

Sometimes it appears to be simpler to adore others than to cherish yourself, however, self-acknowledgment is an essential piece of building solid associations with others. Luckily, with a little arrangement and development, you can likewise find out how to cherish yourself.

Build Up Your Inner Voice

Resolve negative convictions about yourself. The vast majority experience difficulty relinquishing the negative considerations they have about themselves. Such adverse considerations additionally originate from outside individuals whose conclusions we regard and from whom we look for affection and acknowledgment.

Avoid hairsplitting. Numerous individuals experience issues remembering anything short of perfection from themselves. In the event that you end up looking for compulsiveness and getting awful about yourself when you're not exactly perfect, make three straightforward strides. Stop the present line of reasoning. At that point, focus on the responsibility expected to progress in the direction of a target, and afterward include the exertion required.

Moving your consideration from the last item (which can be decided regarding "flawlessness") to the dedication behind a vocation (which is increasingly hard to measure as "great") will assist you with valuing your own great work.

Dispose of the negative channel. Focusing on life-long issues is a negative pattern of behavior. Unreasonable emphasis on horrifying or less tempting lifelong occasions that make such occasions too critical. When you end up believing that everything that transpires is terrible, try to find a little proof despite what you might expect; it is extremely rare that it is truly terrible. Always call yourself names. Calling yourself a name transforms you from a person to a single element of yourself that you don't like.

- Saying "I'm such a loser" after being fired from a career is wrong and unfair to you. Instead, make a helpful statement, "I lost my job, but I can use this vision to find and keep a new job." To think that "I am too stupid" is also plausible and reductive." Don't believe the worst will happen. It can be easy to assume that each scenario produces the worst result. However, adjusting your inner thoughts rationally or honestly will help you avoid the generalization or misunderstanding that results from the worst.
- Now edit your internal file.
- Consider the list very unique.
- Give yourself the luxury of your life.
- Celebrate and praise yourself for it.

Build a strategy to deal with failures or disappointments. Consider what threatens you to move away from your new course of self-love and decide whether to deal with such things. You understand that you cannot influence the words and deeds of others, however, you can regulate your emotions and responses.

You may find that the adverse observations of a specific individual, such as your mother or boss, are putting you in a spiral of pessimism. When this happens consistently, try to understand that it is so. Conclude how you will manage the negative emotions you have. You may need to be given the opportunity to meditate or relax. Perceive your feelings and transform your negative reactions into a productive fortification of your trust.

Visit your psychiatrist. Investigating negative considerations and discovering the purposes behind your feelings can arouse emotions or encounters from your past that are difficult to manage.

A therapist who has experience dealing with the traumatic past will help you get through the healing process without allowing you to relive difficult memories.

A therapist's office can be a great place to learn how to treat your negative thoughts productively and recognize your positive qualities.

Make Positive Statements Every Day

Identify those positive considerations that will help you feel more grounded and check them consistently.

A decent positive statement to cultivate self-esteem is: "I am a whole, commendable individual, and I respect, trust and love myself." If you find that validations don't help isolate, try visiting a consultant and looking for an astonishing treatment that also joins various systems.

Get involved in things that make you happy and feel excited. Take what it takes to feel positive in various ways; it may include yoga, reflection, dance and maintaining a positivity diary. Find a program that makes you feel comfortable and respect it.

Do not hesitate to take advantage of the time alone and enjoy it!

Reflect on the results of self-love. When you spend time having fun and supporting yourself, you are sure to find results in other aspects of your life. Note if you have more time or if you can be more collaborative with others. You may begin to feel that you are more responsible for the choices you make and have more control over your life.

Practice Meditation

Identify adverse reactions to positive statements that you have. If you have pessimistic thoughts when hearing these affirmations, avoid what causes those negative thoughts. Identify people you have difficulty expressing true love for. Repeat your comments and talk about these people.

Dream of someone you're feeling good about. Repeat the statements and keep the person in mind while you repeat them.

Talk of someone you are not indifferent to. Repeat the affirmations, bearing in mind the person you feel indifferent about.

Enable the affirmations to fill you absolutely with positivity. Repeat the affirmations without actually speaking about anyone. Rather emphasize on the positivity of the claims. Enable the positivity feelings to fill you totally and take the positivity out to the entire world from yourself.

Repeat one more love chant. When you've expanded positivity thoughts everywhere, utter the following mantra: "Let all living human beings experience and be good, and safe." Utter this phrase five times as you hear the words echo in your body and reach out to everyone throughout the world.

Understand Self-Love

Realizing the risks of an absence of self-esteem. Lack of self-esteem can lead you to make dangerous decisions. The absence of self-esteem also equates to an absence of self-respect which adds to conscious or unaware self-harm and prevents individuals from taking care of their main needs.

The absence of self-esteem may require negative certification for others. According to others, persistence also allows people to put aside their desires in order to collect the help of others.

The absence of self-esteem can also frustrate mental recovery and progress; an investigation found that individuals who enjoy self-love and ignore each other have more unpleasant results.

See the estimate of early experiences in creating some great memories. Father-son affiliations have long-lasting ramifications for character progression; children who have not met physical, social and lead needs may have long-lasting problems with little certainty.

The antagonistic messages reached the young people – in particular the monotonous messages – regularly bind to the individual's brain and influence their acknowledgments along the way.

For example, a young man who is informed that he is "boring" or "grueling" will likely imagine he is boring or grueling as an adult, regardless of whether there is evidence despite what one might expect, (for example, having a lot of companions, make people laugh or have a fascinating way of life).

See how guardians should cultivate trust. Guardians should follow the accompanying advice to help their young people's confidence: tune in to their children; expanding their trust.

It may very well be quick to "freeze" a child who gets busy, who generally does not tune in to what he does. In any case, in case you really listen to him and talk to him/her asking him subsequent questions and noting his comments, he may realize that you consider what he needs are.

Show children in a non-forced way (without punching, screaming or abuse) to improve their safety.

For example, if your child hits another child, you should bring him to the side and gently remind him that he should not touch other children or that he may be injured. If necessary, you can take a short break to relax and regroup before returning to play.

Offer comfort, compassion, support and respect to children without judgment to make them feel worthy of love and acceptance.

If that child of yours reveals that he is irritated by something that seems strange to you (like the setting sun), do not give up his feelings. Recognize his feelings by saying, "I understand why you are disturbed in light of the fact that the sun has set. Then do your best to justify that the situation cannot be reversed by saying something like," The sun has to go down every night because the world turns and people on the other side of the planet need the sun. It also gives us the opportunity to relax and prepare for the day. "In the end, extend a hug or other physical affection and console the child to let him know that you are empathizing with him/her even if you cannot change the situation. Understand the effects of external feedback on love for yourself. You will experience disappointment in your self-love cannot be made in a vacuum without the inside.

The Fourth Phase: Making a Wise Decision

Did you know that the laws of motion can be applied to your relationship? Yes, I am not joking, and it is true! The first law of motion states that an object will not move until an external force is applied. The second law states that an object will accelerate only when an external force is applied. The third law of motion states that every action has an equal and opposite reaction. These are three simple laws and can be easily applied to any relationship. By applying the first law of motion, you will realize that your relationship will continue to exist the way it is and will not change unless you make any changes. This applies to things both good as well as bad. For instance, if you are tired of the way you both deal with arguments, then this pattern will not change unless you both make a conscious effort to make the change. According to the second law of motion, you cannot make any changes unless you make a conscious decision to do so and put in the necessary effort. The third law of motion is perhaps the most easily explainable one. The way you act influences the way your partner reacts. Now, the same concepts can be used for setting goals in your relationship as well. When you set goals, it gives your relationship the required momentum to keep going. When you and your partner come up with certain mutually agreeable goals to improve your relationship, you can create an assignment that is conducive to your relationship's growth. The goals you set will help avoid your relationship getting stagnant. Setting goals is quite easy, and the chances of success in attaining these goals increase when you set simple goals. The relationship goals you come up with will help you and your partner concentrate on your relationship even when you hit a rough patch. Once you come up with goals, you must make sure that you are both willing to put in the necessary effort to attain them. Establish goals yourself and allow your partner to do the same. You can sit down together, brainstorm, and come up with relationship goals for your relationship together.

Make it a point to set goals about communication, love, compromise, commitment, sexual intimacy, household chores, and support. These are the main aspects that influence the quality and strength of your relationship. Once you cover these areas and come up with attainable goals, you can improve and strengthen your relationship.

It is quintessential that you and your partner both work on improving the way you communicate with each other. While setting goals in this area, think about ways in which you can improve your communication. To do this, go through the different tips related to communication in this.

Take some time, sit down with your partner, and asked them what they need. Emotional support is not the only form of support you can provide your partner with. At times, something as simple as driving your partner to the grocery store or taking those to the dentist are forms of support too. Make sure that you set some time aside to check in with your partner regularly.

For a relationship to last, then there needs to be friendship in it. You must be more than just partners; you must be friends first. Come up with different things you and your partner can do together. Shared activity certainly helps increase your degree of closeness. In fact, you and your partner can also take turns to select different activities you can try out together.

I am certain you love your partner, but how expressive are you? If you don't express your love, how will your partner ever know? How often do you express your thoughts? I'm not suggesting that you need to keep telling your partner over and over again that you love them, but there are little things you can do which convey your love for them. For instance, sharing in on any household responsibilities, cooking their favorite meal, or giving them a hug as soon as you wake up in the morning are all ways in which you can show your love for them. In a long-term relationship, it is quintessential that you express your love and affection for your partner.

A relationship will not last if there are no compromises. My way or the highway kind of thinking can quickly shatter any relationship. Instead, learn to compromise. It is okay if you don't always get your way, and it is okay if you are not always right. Start making an effort to understand your partner's perspective. Learn to negotiate and understand the importance of coming to compromises. When you compromise, it doesn't mean that you are wrong while your partner is right, it merely means that you love your partner more and are willing to concentrate on the relationship instead of any other petty issues or problems.

Emotional intimacy is as important as physical intimacy in a relationship. So, make a conscious effort and set certain goals for physical intimacy in your relationship. Be a responsive and caring lover to your partner. Spend some time and discuss with your partner about all the various things you want to try and be open with them. Learn to cater to not just your needs, but the needs of your partner as well.

A common problem a lot of couples run into is related to household responsibilities. I believe in the equality of partners, and therefore partners must share all responsibilities. After all, you are living together, so why not share the responsibilities? Spend some time and come up with a schedule to divide responsibilities between the two of you so that one partner doesn't always feel burdened with household work. This is quintessential, especially if you and your partner have day jobs to attend to as well.

Tips To Keep In Mind

Happiness doesn't always come from getting what you want, but it can come from moving toward what you desire. When it comes to relationships, it essentially means that couples must have a couple of goals they are moving toward together. So, how can couples support and motivate each other to achieve their individual goals along with the relationship goals? Well, here are some simple steps you can follow to ensure that you and your partner reach your goals while maintaining the health of your relationship.

The first step is to ensure that your individual goals are in perfect alignment with your relationship goals. This alignment is quintessential to create a sense of harmony, which allows you both to attain your personal goals. Once this harmony is present, there is no limit to the things you can both achieve together as a team.

It is time to make two plans - a six-month plan and a two-year plan. Think of this as short and long-term goals for your relationship. Have a discussion about what you plan on doing, where you want to be, and how you want to be within these two timeframes. The following step is to visualize and think about where you want your life to be in the continuing five, 10, 15, and 20 years. Ensure that you both maintain a positive attitude, and don't casually write off any ideas until you have both had a chance to express yourself first. Don't judge your partner, and don't allow your partner to judge you. Keep an open mind toward each other and attentively listen to what the other person has to say.

Spend some time and make a list of all your personal goals. You and your partner must do this individually and then spend some time together to discuss the lists you both made. You can take all the time you need, and carefully note down everything you wish to attain in life. Include short-term as well as long-term goals and discuss this if you feel like you're getting stuck while making this list.

Whenever you are setting any goals, the goals must be such that they make you feel good about yourself. If the goal you are setting for yourself or for your relationship goes against everything you believe in, you will not be able to achieve it. The goals you set for yourself must not only be good for you but must be good for your relationship as well. When you have shared goals, it not only becomes easier to achieve them, but the health of your relationship also improves along the way.

Regardless of the goal you set, make sure that the goals are specific, realistic, and attainable. If a goal doesn't fulfill even one of these conditions, then you are merely setting yourself up for failure. People often think that setting lofty goals for themselves is a good idea. They seem to stand by the age-old adage of, "If you shoot for the stars, you will land on the moon." Well, I don't think this is the right way to go about setting goals. After all, if you don't attain your goals, it will be a source of massive disappointment and discontent. To avoid this, ensure that the goals you are setting are realistic, attainable, and quite specific.

You and your partner must come up with an arrangement that helps you stay focused and accountable for any commitments you make to each other. The relationship you share with your partner is quite sacred, and you must cherish and nourish it. The arrangements you create must support you and your partner along with your relationship. It's not about getting rewards or punishments to create accountability. It is about coming up with a mutually beneficial plan to create accountability to each other.

It is okay to concentrate on your goals, but it is not okay to overlook any victories you attain along the way. Attaining your goals is seldom a sprint and is always a marathon. So, the journey to your goals matters as much as the goal itself. You and your partner must be appreciative of each other and each other's accomplishments. Rejoice in all the small wins that happen in your lives. Celebrate each other's successes. By doing this, you are naturally cementing the bond you share. If you celebrate every milestone you cross, it will give you the motivation to keep going.

Be each other's support system. There will be days when you or your partner simply don't have the motivation to keep going. In such instances, be each other's cheerleaders. Your relationship will be happier and more satisfactory when you know you have your partner's support, and the same applies to your partner too. In fact, make it a point to seek feedback from your partner to see how they are doing. By asking for their feedback, you are not only making them feel important but are also giving yourself a chance to view things from a fresh perspective.

Make Your Choice

Everyone comes standardly equipped with the internal resources necessary to make the kind of transformation that Chloe did—from hopeless, to optimistic, to joyful. Until now, you might not have been aware of your powers. That doesn't mean you haven't been using them. You have. You've just been using them on the default settings. That is, up to this point, they have been deploying based on your predominant unexamined thoughts. How do you know if this is true? Look around. If your life is short of what your dreams are for yourself, you have an opportunity to explore using your super powers on purpose.

Your first super power is awareness—knowing that "today's you" has tremendous power to make things better for "future you." This is a simple, but very exciting, concept. What's new about this idea is using it in this moment. That means understanding that your life, right this minute, is the culmination of your past beliefs, feelings, thoughts and actions. All of your power is RIGHT NOW. What you believe, think and do now has more impact on your future reality than anything in your past.

Doing things for yourself now takes care of you now. You can enjoy the current moment for what it is while also setting future you up for more joy. Awareness is powerful because it's the gateway into choice, your super power. It's an essential ingredient of change. It's the awareness that you have the power to create something different for yourself if you choose to, starting now.

Recently divorced and feeling a little stuck, my client Ken got intrigued by this idea. He worked in a job that he didn't enjoy and the days were flying by without him making any forward motion toward his dreams. He didn't know what to do so he did nothing. Today's Ken was setting future Ken up for more of the same.

As we worked together, he started to become more aware that doing nothing was actually decision by indecision. He was making a passive choice, but it was a choice just the same. It hit home with him that, whether he did anything about it or not, he did have choices. Once that awareness took root, he made the decision to put some of his focus on exploring his options (which, coincidently, is the super power).

You can have awareness, but unless you're willing to direct some of your focus and attention to what you want, you'll stay where you are. So, focus works hand in hand with awareness and choice. (Your time reading this is a great example of putting your focus on what you want to create for yourself.)

A stressed-out single mom, Sienna was pretty clear that she wanted to feel calmer and more peaceful. After doing some research, she decided that trying meditation might be beneficial. Her biggest issue was time. When we started working together, her two kids and full-time job kept her very busy. I really understood her situation. And, I still felt that she could find some time to focus on what she wanted.

When we looked at her schedule, it became clear she was using binge-watching TV and internet surfing to try and de-stress after her kids went to bed. Unfortunately, this strategy left her more tired, a little depressed and just as stressed. She committed to carving out five minutes a night, before she started on TV, to try a guided meditation. She found it very relaxing and it soon became a habit.

After a few weeks, she started supplementing her evening meditation by reading a few pages of an uplifting instead of automatically turning to TV. Now, she still has TV shows she likes, and that's fine. But, she watches a show or two and then turns off the set. She still meditates and she's found a deep reserve of calm she never knew she had, all because she was willing to shift some of her focus to what she wanted to create for herself.

Like Sienna, you are creating your life moment by moment. You're aware you have the choice to change things for yourself starting this minute. You're willing to focus your attention on doing it.

The super power, intention, is about directing the first three powers toward what you want. Intentions are proactive decisions about how you're going to "show up"—inside yourself and outside in the world. Your intentions lead to inspired thoughts and actions that create forward momentum toward what you want.

Living on Purpose

Intention-setting is not about dogged determination or forcing yourself to succeed at all costs. It's the process of deciding what it is you want and getting a clear picture of it.

So, what does all of this have to do with your divorce or breakup? Good question! Without a doubt, setting intentions is a powerful tool for both inner peace and outer results in any part of your life. However, for our purposes, we're going to focus on setting post-divorce intentions. So, let's start with a few guidelines.

- Be positive and affirming—Your intentions should say what you want, not what you don't want. For example:
  - Weak Intention: My intention is not to get angry or anxious when I meet with my Ex.
  - Powerful Intention: I intend to breathe deeply to help me relax and to calmly hold my boundaries when I meet with my Ex.
- Assume success—Don't build qualifiers into your intentions. For example:
  - Weak Intention: My intention is to remain peaceful inside myself when my Ex picks up the kids, as long as he's on time.
  - Powerful Intention: My intention is to remain peaceful inside myself when my Ex picks up the kids.

Come from your values and beliefs— Strive to get in touch with the deepest and truest part of yourself and set your intentions from that place.

After his second wife moved out, Ken was deeply hurt and full of anger. How could this have happened again? After the worst of the shock wore off, he decided to use the experience to grow as a person.

He realized that after his first marriage ended, he had jumped fairly quickly into dating without much reflection. Being single was uncomfortable for him and he fell into the relationship that became his second marriage.

With two divorces under his belt, Ken set his intention to learn about his own unconscious relationship patterns. He also set his intention to move from judgment and bitterness to forgiveness and acceptance. His sister, who was his closest confidant, was still very angry and didn't understand his desire to move past the rage. Thankfully, Ken was true to himself and based his intentions on his own inner guidance rather than his sister's influence.

It paid off. With the help of a therapist, he learned about his unconscious need for approval that led to him marrying two women with many of the same characteristics. Armed with this self-knowledge, he made a list of requirements for the qualities he wanted in a life partner. Three years, he's in a committed relationship with someone who's a great fit for him.

Another one of my clients, Barb, had an Ex who was habitually late picking up their kids. As the agreed-on time came and went, she could feel herself becoming very worked up. By the time he arrived, she would be upset and so would the kids. This inevitably started a nasty scene. She realized this amount of stress wasn't good for her or her kids and she set the intention to let go of taking it personally. Her Ex had always been looser about the definition of "on time" than she was. And, maybe it really was a passive-aggressive move on his part. So what? She couldn't control how he conducted his life. What she could control was how she responded. Her intention was to transform waiting into action.

If she didn't have somewhere else to be at the scheduled pick-up time, her chosen action was to just let it go. That by itself was liberating. In the most practical sense, it had little impact on her if her kids were playing in their rooms waiting for their dad while she zoomed through her household to-do list or relaxed with a magazine. If she did have plans, she came up with another strategy. She often took the kids with her, letting her Ex know where to pick them up. So, instead of putting off running errands until he got there, she took the kids along. Many times, he would show up halfway through a grocery shopping trip and take them from there. Or, in the instances when taking them along wasn't possible, she dropped them with a neighbor to keep an eye on them until he arrived.

At first, her friends thought she was crazy for what they perceived as letting him off the hook. But Barb's inner guidance was clear: her anger was hurting her much more than it hurt him. When she set her intentions, it opened up space for creative problem solving. He was still "hit and miss" with the timing, but her blood pressure was no longer rising to dangerous levels over it. In fact, she was proud of herself for coming up with solutions that met her needs instead of continuing to marinate in aggravation, frustration and rage.

The Fifth Phase: Reconnection

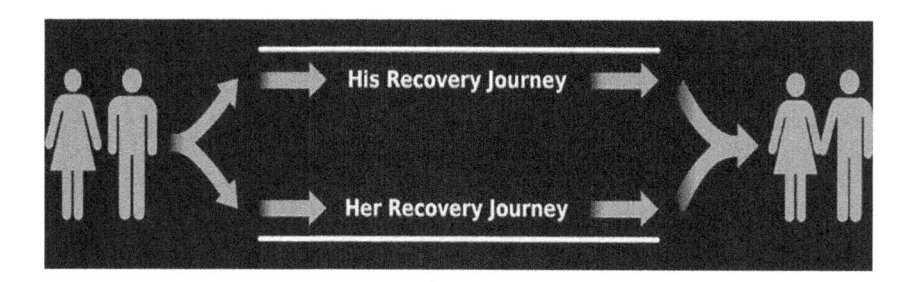

How can you Trust Again?

As a person who has been cheated on, what happened is degrading and unacceptable. You will find yourself asking why, and you might even blame yourself for it. You might think that you are not good enough and that you don't deserve to be loved. This pain shall go on, and memories of that painful experience will keep coming back to you if you don't move on. You will only be able to forget the pain if you allow yourself to heal, and you will only be able to save your relationship if you allow yourself to forgive.

It will be easier for you to heal from betrayal if you avoid bringing back the past. First, it will just cause old wounds to open up again; and second, it may cause a misunderstanding between you and your partner. You've surely fought enough when you first found out about his infidelity, bringing back these memories after a long time might bring back these old fights. Most importantly, you won't be able to take one step forward and leave it all behind if you keep reminding yourself of what happened in the past. Even though it is something that should not be forgotten, you must not bring it back over and over again for new memories to take its place. Eventually, it will become a lesson for you and your partner and a mistake that must not be done yet.

As a lesson that you and your partner must've learned by now, remember to keep an open line of communication between the two of you because you must've realized by now how vital communication is in a relationship. Always talk things through no matter how nasty the situation gets because it is through talking to each other that you will be able to understand the cause of the problem and its probable solutions.

Lastly, if you want to heal, then do not be paranoid. This may be a tough thing to do, mainly because you have already experienced being cheated on, but it is something that you must strive for if you want to move on. Even if it's hard, you must learn how to trust your partner again. They say trust is earned and not given, so the better thing to do is to exert willingness to trust your partner again. Give him room to improve and to prove himself. Do not be too paranoid of all his actions – believe that he will not do it again and take his word for it.

Trying to forget such a painful phase in your life is very difficult, but surely you can do it! It just takes a lot of courage and willingness, and eventually, you'll find yourself looking back at something that once caused you pain but has now made you stronger and wiser

How to regain your partner's trust

This is dedicated to the one who has made a mistake of betraying their partner. Restoring your partner's faith is not an easy task; you must know that you're in for a challenging journey. But remember that this journey may be full of challenges, and there will be times that you will feel like giving up, but what's more important is the prize at the end, and that is a strengthened relationship with your partner.

First things first – if you wish to regain your partner's trust, then the first thing that you must do is to take full responsibility for your mistakes. Don't go, "I did it because you did this and that!" on your partner, it will only make things worse. Remember that the decision to commit infidelity came from you and you alone, you could've suppressed it, but you did not. However, take this as a lesson and own up to your mistakes. Show your partner that you are deeply sorry for what happened and that you realize what wrong you have done.

After owning up to your mistakes, the step is for you to apologize and promise never to do it again. Say the sincerest apology that you could ever muster and mean every word of it. However, a mere excuse is not enough. The more critical part of this apology is the promise that you will not commit the same mistake again. At first, your partner might be doubtful of your words, but if you show her that you meant what you said and that you are living up to your promise, then there should be no doubt that your partner will trust you again. It will take a lot of work, but as long as you meant everything you said, then your hard work will surely reap positive results.

Another thing that you must keep in mind if you wish to regain your partner's trust is to be completely honest with your feelings. Do not keep things from your partner anymore, most especially if it concerns your relationship. Lying to your partner won't do you any good. If your partner observes that you are completely honest with her again, she will learn to trust you again, and she will also eventually start opening up to you again. Maintain this culture of honesty within your relationship, and this will inevitably lead to the return of trust between you and your spouse.

Love and long-term relationship

To tend to a relationship that has been bruised by betrayal, pain, and distrust is difficult and takes a lot of sacrifice, understanding, and determination. Instances of infidelity in a relationship are something that can be easily shrugged off. It is the worst thing that could happen to two lovers. However, if both sides agree to settle their differences, let go of the pain of the past, and move forward together, then definitely they will develop a strengthened relationship filled with lessons from the past.

The continued existence of a love relationship, satisfying and exciting to both partners in the post-affair marriage, is no accident. It involves becoming aware of your needs, of what you want in your relationship, and of letting your spouse know in a caring way. It requires that you let him know what statements and actions hurt your feelings or make you angry. Loving again also includes being sensitive to your partner's needs and encouraging him to express them. Finally, it means accepting your spouse for what he is, an imperfect human being like yourself.

Rebuilding trust	➢ Follow through ➢ Avoid Emotional Triggers ➢ Communicate! ➢ Be realistic ➢ Take your time
Embracing self-forgiveness	
The ways to proactively build trust in your relationship.	➢ Awareness of your partner's emotion ➢ Turning toward the emotion ➢ Tolerance of two different viewpoints ➢ Try to understand your partner ➢ Responding with empathy
The tasks of the betrayed	➢ Ask questions that help you understand the

	meaning, and the motives
The tasks of the unfaithful	➢ Freely admitting fault ➢ Fully accepting responsibilities ➢ Humbly asking for forgiveness ➢ Immediately changing behavior

Embracing Self - Forgiveness

What is Forgiveness?

Forgiveness as a basis for self-healing

When people interact, there will always be events that are appropriate for one and not for the other. There will sometimes be someone who causes pain and someone who gets hurt. There will be things that don't suit one or the other. Our culture encourages the offender to ask for forgiveness. In the Jewish religion there is a time, the holiest day of all, dedicated to the search for forgiveness - Yom Kippur.

Tolerance – the ability to forgive others and ourselves is necessary if we want peace and health. This is our own process with ourselves (sometimes with external help) to forgive, to let go, to free ourselves from the oppression that binds us. Non-forgiveness, resentment, and anger about something that happened to us or what someone did to us are a cause of many diseases.

Life flows on. The essence of life flows through each of us every moment. If we do not forgive, we block the flow of life. We block ourselves and cause ourselves to get "stuck" in what happened. When we do this, we are punishing ourselves, not the one who harmed us. Forgiveness and non-forgiveness are, in fact, two sides of the same coin.

Forgiveness - For the Forgiver

Forgiveness is for the forgiver, not for those who are forgiven. What does forgiveness do for us? When someone does not forgive, that state of "non-forgiveness" resides within them. They are full of anger, frustration and bitterness, conditions which can be harmful to one's health. Forgiveness is necessary for healing. As opposed to someone who stubbornly holds a grudge, if we forgive, we will immediately be relieved, and it will be evident, in the way we feel and in our behavior.

It is important that we understand that it is worth the effort to forgive, not because the offender "deserves it," but for ourselves. If I forgive another, then I can let go and fly higher.

Lack of forgiveness

- Negative indicators: resentment, anger, frustration, bitterness
- Causes physical and mental illness, dissatisfaction, anger, violence, war.

Forgiveness

- Positive indicators: relief, happiness, health
- Liberation, progress, negotiations, reconciliation, love.

The Meaning of Forgiveness in Our Lives

A. Forgiveness as a gift to someone else: Someone has done us wrong, maybe as a result of our behavior. And now the question is whether we will be generous, give the gift of forgiveness or will we be stingy, and not grant forgiveness?

B. Forgiveness as a gift to oneself: Forgiveness is, in fact, a gift we give to ourselves. Forgiveness of another frees us from pain and suffering. It releases us from our prison.

C. Control: We feel that withholding forgiveness keeps us in control, and that if we forgive, we lose control. Since a state of "no-control" is associated with uncertainty, we avoid forgiveness so as to avoid uncertainty.

D. Negative Gain: If I am angry and hold on to that anger by not forgiving, it is as if I "have something on" the other. I control them. But this is a negative gain. Yes, I am the jailer, but like the prisoner, I am also stuck in prison with them.

E. Liberation of the soul: If we forgive, we can free ourselves from our prison.

Understanding the Process of Forgiveness

When I withhold my forgiveness, I live in a prison, in a place that causes me pain. In fact, while I focus on the person I am blaming, and not on myself, I can never get out of this prison. The following question arises: How much am I willing to release, as opposed to how much do I want to keep inside me?

Conditions necessary for forgiveness

In order for us to carry out the process of forgiveness, we must fulfill certain conditions within ourselves. We must be able to:

1. Identify the type of "shell" we're wearing

When we get hurt, we tend to put on a protective shell. People interpret and respond to events they encounter in different ways. We give events a personal meaning. Some respond with anger, fear, hurt, loneliness, accusation, sadness, despair, or frustration. Some people embrace the identity of victims, some become analytic, and some avoid all response. People attach meaning to events and take things to heart in different ways. Everything angers the angry person; everything frightens the frightened person. The aching person is vulnerable and always lives in pain. The sad person lives sadly. The desperate lives in despair and guilt, and so on.

Each of us develops his or her own outer shell in accordance with our specific responses. We wear a shell to protect our true selves.

It is very important for each of us to clearly understand the shell we wear to protect ourselves, to hide our inner selves from others. That shell is part of our unforgiving state. We need to ask ourselves, what's in there? What's happening under my shell?

2. Be prepared to peel off the shell

Giving up on our shell is a frightening step. Am I ready for this? Am I ready to see what's underneath? Am I willing to forgive? Am I willing to give up the notion that forgiveness means betraying myself?

What will happen to me if I give up my shell?

- Will I lose anything?

- Will I become someone else?

It is not easy. If I give up my shell, I'll have to face the person who hurt me, naked and exposed. I'll become someone who behaves, responds, feels differently from what I am accustomed to. It'll make me feel like I'm losing myself, and therefore, it frightens me. We know that removing the shell will cause the person facing us to behave differently toward us, which is also frightening, very frightening.

In spite of the fear, the uncertainty of how we will manage without the shell, it is important to continue the process.

3. Stop blaming - release from guilt - forgive

In order to forgive we have to stop blaming! For some, it is a chronic pleasure to blame and to live in a drama. Blaming has great power. Blaming frees you from having to look at yourself. We love to blame because it's easier for us to blame another when something goes wrong. "It's because of her…she's guilty; I'm angry because she angered me; I'm offended because she insulted me." We live in a drama.

The trick is to stop the blaming. Just let it go! To understand that "it takes one to know one," every time we see a fault in another it's a sign that we've got the same fault.

If it's hard for us to bear the behavior of someone, then it's often because we have the same behavioral tendency. In fact, it's hard for us to bear ourselves. So, the way to deal with this issue is to release the other from guilt, and to take a look at the same issue within ourselves.

It is hard for us to stop blaming because we fall into our assumptions, our desires, into negative ego. Basic assumptions are very dangerous. People think they are right only because of their basic assumptions. The way to be free is to erase our basic assumptions. The point is, it's very hard to find our basic assumptions on our own.

- Am I willing to let go of the justifiable excuses to keep the resentment?
- Am I willing to stop being stubborn?
- Am I willing to let go of blaming others?
- Am I willing to let go of blaming myself? If I stop blaming, I will shift the focus from the other to myself.

4. Map the layers of our shells

Shells come in layers. Each of us has a wide spectrum of inner layers, shells over shells, like an onion. Having agreed to give up the outer shell, we stopped saying what bothers us in the other; now it's time to get inside ourselves and identify our own inner layers.

It is not always easy to identify these shells. These are dominant emotions that have become part of our lives and are therefore difficult to identify. The layers are our masks. Each of us wears a different mask on different occasions. We need to identify and understand the layers and to be willing to give up the false sense of security they give us.

5. Begin peeling away layers

Having identified the layers, we now must decide what to give up. It is not easy. This can be likened to sitting in the cinema, when someone blocks our view. It is easier for us to ask to the person in front of us to move right or left than to move ourselves.

- Do I want to give up?
- Am I ready to give up? If not, then ask yourself:
- Why is it hard for me to let go, to release?
- What negative gain do I have from resisting forgiveness?

6. Release the fears of the past

We identified the layers, and let them go, and what now?

Now we are in a state of fear that everything will repeat itself, that we'll suffer the same violation again. And the moment arrives when we need to overcome the fear. Clinging to the past prevents us from forgiving. In order to get rid of this dependence on the past, we must identify and overcome our fears. Ask yourself:

- Am I afraid of loneliness?
- Am I afraid not being appreciated?
- Am I afraid of death?
- Am I afraid of public speaking?

Releasing the past means accepting and internalizing the past, leading to forgiveness and growth.

Rebooting Your Relationship

Restoring your relationship after an affair can feel like the most difficult task in your life. In some ways, I am happy for you that you find this period in your life difficult, and here is why I say that: If the process were easy, you would be more likely to repeat the offense. You know it, and so do I, so let's just get honest about why we are here so we can get on with the activities that can improve your relationship patterns.

In the 7 Step Infidelity Recovery Program, the couple completes a series of 'monologues' on their personal history and their relationship history. The idea is to have the couple relearn each other from scratch. Now if you were to think about it, when you were dating and courting your spouse, were you 100 percent honest about your history, your background, you're real thoughts on 'hot' topics, and everything else about yourself? Even if you were 100 percent honest at that time, are you the same person now? The better question is: Have you shared your inner thoughts, feelings, and events with your spouse over the years?

Remember: If your spouse knew everything about you, then you would not have had an affair!

Infidelity Recovery is the perfect opportunity to rebuild the relationship. You must restore the friendship and learn how to communicate with respect, empathy, laughter, and love. Falling in love was easy to do, because you had a growing friendship. You were trying to understand the other person. You were avoiding behavior that might upset them or make them think less of you. Staying in love is what some writers term a labor of love, because you need to work at it!

The love banks

When you were dating, all the good things you were doing were being stored in what we call The Love Bank. We each have a love bank for each person in our life. If someone makes you feel good, then credits are deposited. If that person makes you feel bad, a withdrawal is taken. So over the years, many withdrawals and deposits are made.

Sadly, everything seems to fall down at some point, especially without support, and those balances in the Love Bank are no exception. When the credits reach a certain threshold, the feeling of romantic love is triggered. When the withdrawals reach a certain level, feelings of dislike or hate are triggered.

Couples can soon discover that the feelings of love and romance that they carried into marriage are much more fragile than they ever imagined while dating. Eventually, they lose all their passion and their instinctive desire to make each other happy. Their Love Bank balances drop way below their threshold levels for romance. What once seemed easy and effortless becomes awkward and hateful; apathy replaces the 'look of love.' Bereaved of love, the husband and the wife want to spend their lives apart, and sometimes go on to divorce.

It should be clear to you by now that this whole Love Bank thing matters in every marriage. If you want to stay married for life, with your emotions and instincts supported, the Love Bank balance must stay above the romantic threshold levels. You might be wondering: How can you keep the balances that high? What should you do if the balances are already dropping below the threshold levels?

I worked hard for a long time to find answers to those questions, since they form the roots of any marriage. When love feels absent, couples are less motivated to stay together for life. When love is restored, the emotions and the instincts to stay together come back. This restoration means not only that divorces are avoided, but also that marriages are enriched for the long haul and families remain intact.

All of the aforementioned basic concepts revolve around those questions, but the general principle is simple and solid: If you and your partner want to be happily married forever, the two of you should keep your Love Bank balances above the threshold levels and keep withdrawals as low as possible.

This can be achieved by changing the way you behave. It doesn't mean being selfless all the time; however, when you behave in ways that you know will increase your partner's happiness and avoid behaviors that result in your partner's unhappiness, you are creating a positive balance in your relationship and making it more likely that your partner will do the same.

Love busters

Why do we hurt the one we promised to love and care for at all times? Often, the core of the problem is our lack of empathy. Many spouses who grumble about how inconsiderate their partners are fail to realize they are being inconsiderate as well. Apathy triggers thoughtlessness, allowing you to behave in inconsiderate ways. When we do not understand or consider how others feel, we tend to ignore the negative effects we have on others and consider our thought lessens to be benign. Your partner's reaction may be a strong message that he/she needs more thought from you, not less.

People regard their own angry outbursts as creative expression and think their disrespect will help their partners gain proper perspective. They consider demands to be nothing more than encouraging a spouse to do what he or she should have done all along. These acts aren't considered hurtful or thoughtless by the one inflicting the pain. But eventually, all these things will cause Love Bank withdrawals.

Dr. Willard Harley, founder of Marriage Builders, applies the term Love Busters to behaviors that cause Love Bank withdrawals. These behaviors fit six basic categories, according to Dr. Harley:

1. Selfish Demands

2. Disrespectful Judgments

3. Angry Outbursts

4. Annoying Habits

5. Independent Behavior

6. Dishonesty.

The first three Love Busters are instinctive, thoughtless methods to try to get what you want from each other, according to Dr. Harley. In cases where requests are denied, a spouse will go to the demand mode: "I don't care how you feel—do it or else!" If that doesn't work, a spouse will become disrespectful and judgmental: "If you had any sense, and were not so lazy and selfish, you would do it." Finally, when nothing else gets the job done, an angry outburst comes as the last resort: "I'll make sure you regret not doing it."

When your spouse does what you want as a way to return the care and consideration you have shown, the Love Bank balance increases. When you use demands, disrespect, and anger to get your way, your spouse may be more likely to ignore your requests or push back, meaning the tactic has backfired. And what about when this behavior works? When your partner gives you what you want only because you resorted to Love Busters, getting your way comes with a terrible cost—a withdrawal from the Love Bank, a decrease in caring, an increase in inconsiderate behavior.

Employing these three Love Busters may not only prevent you from getting what you want, but also destroy the love you have for each other. All these instinctive behaviors, and the habits they tend to nurture, result in spousal unhappiness and Love Bank withdrawals.

Annoying Habits, the fourth Love Buster, is the kind of behavior that is so thoughtless and repetitive that it tends to hurt your spouse. Marriage is a partnership of incredibly close quarters, where even small behaviors impact the other person. If you expect to stay in love with each other, your habits, even the innocent ones, should cause Love Bank deposits rather than withdrawals.

Independent Behavior, the fifth Love Buster, is the kind of behavior and conduct of one partner that ignores the feelings and interests of the other partner. The independent decisions that one makes while ignoring the partner's needs and ignoring or not allowing input from the partner, result in Love Bank withdrawals because they are hurtful.

Dishonesty, the sixth Love Buster, is a highly damaging behavior. It accounts for the largest of Love Bank withdrawals whenever it's discovered. Do not lie; do not distort the truth; remove dishonesty from your relationship before it's too late. Now is the time for full honesty.

The surveys that follow include multiple questions because there are multiple Love Busters. Try to be honest and fair in your answers to establish a proper rank of the Love Busters.

While all Love Busters should be eliminated, it is logical to focus on particular Love Busters in the beginning. The questionnaires should help you pinpoint the areas of misery and sadness in your marriage. When your behavior leads to sadness and pain, you not only reduce love units, but you provide a reason for your spouse to erect an emotional fence to separate from you emotionally. When your spouse detaches in this way to protect from pain, he/she may have trouble letting you in even when you want to make a love deposit.

It is only by overcoming Love Busters that you can remove the emotional obstacles and accommodate the emotional desires of your spouse. For this reason, your Love Busters should be destroyed before you discover how to meet each other's expectations. Destroying Love Busters allows you to restore passion in your marriage.

Questionnaire

It is normal to upset the one you love sometimes, or to be upset. However, over time, some habits can destroy romantic love and build emotional resistance. While it may protect you from pain, such emotional resistance also can stop you from receiving more love units to compensate for the lost ones. Let's look at the Love Busters impacting your marriage.

- The first step of the questionnaire identifies the things your partner did to increase the Love Bank units.
- The second step identifies the things your partner did to decrease your Love Bank units.
- The third step identifies the things a 'third party' has done to increase the Love Busters.

Each of you should fill in the first three steps as accurately as possible, in order to identify your Love Busters. Put aside your emotions so they don't get in the way or sidetrack you while you complete the questionnaires.

The information gathered in the first three steps will help you each fill in a table that follows. That table will assist you and your partner in identifying whether your Love Bank credits are above or below the threshold level. Step 5 is a 21-day worksheet plan to help you restore your Love Bank credits and get past the threshold level.

The Sixth Phase: Love and Start Again

Communication and quality time are important in a relationship. If you don't have these two ingredients, your relationship will suffer. From years of experience in treating couples and families in therapy, we have compiled effective strategies to improve marriages and relationships. Here are two things to consider.

1. Communicate your needs to your spouse.

Communication is a two-way street. One direction is output (what is being said) and the other direction is input (what is being heard). In the first direction (output), communication is an opportunity to convey your thoughts, feelings, wishes, needs, and goals.

There are some basic rules for effective communication.

The more specific and clear you are, the better your message will be understood. The best way to do this is to use direct, non-judgmental verbal communication. By direct communication, we mean directly to your spouse, not to your friends at work.

Timing is key. Make sure to use appropriate timing. For example, if your spouse is in the middle of an important meeting at work, do not call on his or her cell phone and demand to have a conversation. If you are not sure if the timing is right, it may be helpful to ask your spouse to suggest a good time to discuss needs, wishes, issues, and the like.

A positive tone of voice is most effective, especially when using I-messages.

I-message statements are about yourself or your feelings. They begin with "I feel" or "I felt," instead of blaming statements that start with "you," which are usually followed by negative statements about the person or something he or she did. If your spouse is on the receiving end, he or she will feel attacked or criticized.

As a result, your spouse will most likely deny wrongdoing and maybe start a verbal counterattack. This type of communication can cause a conversation to easily spiral out of control. With I-messages you are simply conveying a problem without blaming anyone for it. By using blame-free communication, you can disarm a potentially escalating conversation. In addition, no one can deny the truthfulness of your feelings, because feelings are subjective, personal, and true to you.

Let's practice using I-messages together. We will show you how to avoid using the word you in an accusatory manner. When people hear you, they tend to get defensive.

For example:

You-messages	I-messages
"You make me feel terrible about myself."	"I feel insecure about myself when we argue."
"I feel hurt because you are inconsiderate."	"I feel hurt when my wishes about spending more time together are ignored."
"You don't listen to me."	"I don't feel heard."
"You broke your promise to take me out on Saturday night."	"I felt disappointed when we didn't go out on Saturday night."

When you use I-messages, you are still conveying the same message but without being accusatory. This is a more effective way of communicating.

"You don't have to like me, but you must respect me." – HARYCE LOMASKY

Exercise

In the following, practice changing your You-messages to I-messages.

You-messages	I-messages

The second direction of communication (input) is listening. Listening is not just hearing with your ears; it is understanding the message that is being conveyed to you.

If you are not sure that the other person understands you, there is a way to find out. Ask your spouse to tell you, in his or her own words, what he or she just understood you said. For example, the wife says, "When you come home from work and finish your dinner, you want to go to sleep and not talk with me or watch TV together." The husband (using this technique) says, "I understand that you don't like it when I go to sleep after dinner because you believe I don't want to spend time with you."

By using this technique, you will be able to validate your spouse's feelings and communicate better, thereby reducing the feelings of anger, sadness, or frustration that you may experience. You will now feel heard and understood by your spouse. This will certainly help with reducing the number of times you tell your spouse something repeatedly. In other words, your message will not go in one ear and out the other.

Don't assume. Remember, assuming that your spouse knows what you are trying to say, or that your spouse should know (after being with you for such a long time) is not reasonable. After all, everyone knows what ASSUME stands for.

It makes an ass out of you and me.

2. Plan a weekly date night.

Date night is a night when the two of you go out together for a special night, to focus on each other without any distractions. This weekly date is marked on the calendar; each spouse will take turns organizing the evening. We suggest implementing the following rules to make date night a success:

- Turn off cell phones.
- No negative discussions about work, sex, finances, or children.
- Talk about anything positive: at the moment, in your week, in the future, in the past (in essence about your passions, dreams, goals, motivations, etc.).

- Make sure to complement each other (For example, tell your spouse how good he/she looks, thank your spouse for planning the evening).
- This evening does not need to end with sex, but try to be intimate in some way.
- Don't go to a place where you just had an argument.
- Try to plan the evening in advance (especially if there are babysitters needed).
- Don't include other couples in date night.
- Don't get drunk on date night (we don't want you to pass out on your spouse).

Some good suggestions for date night are:

- A movie and dinner at a restaurant you know your spouse will like
- A new restaurant
- A show or theatre, with or without dinner
- Candlelight dinner at home (if you have children make sure to arrange for a baby-sitter in advance)
- Listening to live music at a local club
- A concert
- A night in a hotel
- Bowling or playing pool
- A walk on the beach
- Laser tag, paint ball, bungee jumping (if you are an active and thrill-seeking couple)

Exercise

Check the box that indicates what you would like your spouse to do to keep you in the marriage. (We are assuming that you have mastered almost all of these things yourself, right?! If not, we will help guide you...)

- Show a positive mood (smiling more often, using a gentle tone of voice, etc.).
- Express appreciation (thank-you, etc.).
- Give daily compliments.
- Help more with household chores (cleaning, taking trash out, buying groceries, cooking).
- Communicate in a clear, specific, and positive manner.
- Initiate more intimacy (hold my hand, kiss me, hug me...).
- Initiate more/less sex with me.
- Show more interest in my life/my activities (ask questions).
- Listen actively.
- Be more patient.
- Spend more quality time with me.
- Show more affection towards me.
- Attend more to my needs (make a meal for me, bring me a coffee in the morning, etc.).
- Be considerate of my likes and dislikes.

- Bring me a surprise gift once In a while.
- Be more generous towards me.
- Speak positively about me to others.
- Be more respectful towards me.
- Other_____

If You Have Children:

- Help more with the kids (feeding, dressing, bathing, homework, transportation, etc.).
- Spend more quality time with the kids.
- Be on the same page with me in disciplining the kids.
- Attend school meetings and extracurricular activities (i.e., dance lessons, sports, swimming lessons, music lessons, etc.).
- Get up to attend children's needs during the night or in the morning.

Exercises to Reconnect with Your Partner

This will help begin to foster that trust and intimacy that may have degraded over time. It is imperative that you go through this process to ensure that you know not only what you are doing, but how you are doing it. It will help you greatly imagine what it is that really matters and how you can foster it.

Try Something New for Both of You

The first exercise for you to try is to find something that neither of you has done nor work hard to make it happen between both of you. The idea here is that you should both be entirely unfamiliar with what you are about to do. You should both be just as experienced about whatever is happening. It could be that only one of you has any real interest, and that is okay. However, ideally, it would be something that both of you would really enjoy doing.

When you find out what is that you both have never tried together, it is time to make it happen. It is always better if what you are trying is something that will ideally allow for you both to work together—perhaps it is an escape room, which is highly trendy these days and will require teamwork. Maybe you do one of those partner paint activities in which you both paint one half of a scene that is meant to be hung over your bed. No matter what it is that you both decide to do, it should be something that is compelling and brings you both some enjoyment.

After you have tried this new thing together, it is time for you to both talk about it. Talk about how fun it was to experience something together for the first time. Talk about how exciting it was for both of you to get to do something like that and then try to make it happen regularly. You should both try something new often to not only help with your relationship and bonding, but also to help with anxiety as well.

Weekly Date Night

Every week, you should have a date night. It does not matter what the date is—but it should be sacred time for just the two of you to spend time together. Perhaps you decide that you are going to have some date nights at home, and this is fine, too. You do not have to break the bank to have this special time reserved. It could be just as special to cook a nice, special meal, share some wine, and watch a new movie together as it is to go out to a fancy restaurant.

What really matters here, however, is the prioritization of the relationship. Make sure that you are actively putting your relationship first as much as you can to ensure that you are properly taking care of it. It is up to the two of you to maintain your relationship and this is one of the best ways to bring that intimacy and connection back if you have lost touch with it.

Spend Time Together Every Day

Every single day that passes, make it a point to stop and spend time together. It could be that you stop and eat dinner together every night. It could be that you spend some time chatting with your partner in bed without any distractions. It could be that you spend ten minutes each morning cuddling in bed before you get up to face the day, or you spend that time together at night.

There are all sorts of ways to spend time with your partner, even if you are on the go or if you cannot be with each other physically. On the go, you could hold hands in the car as one of you drives, or you could spend time talking, face to face, on a video call if you live too far apart to spend time together regularly. Spend that time together and enjoy that quiet moment together.

Trust Falls

This one may seem kind of doubtful to you—no one likes the idea of falling. However, trust falls are actually legitimately good for your relationship. Your partner should be the first person that you go to when you need something. When you need help, they should be the one that pops into mind. They should be that support for you that you know that you need to ensure that you are able to get that help that is required, and the best way to ensure that you have that is through the use of exercises like this.

The trust fall is meant to be something that will work to establish that trust. Essentially, what you are going to do is stop, lean back, and then allow for the fall to happen. The other person should be right behind your back and ready to catch you when you start to fall. This is essential to ensuring that support for each other. When you do this and when you blindly fall backward, trusting your partner, you will begin to build that trust up. And, if you somehow manage to fall down together, you can laugh and make a joke about it and move on.

Gratitude List

One last exercise for you to consider is the gratitude list. We all have things in our lives that we are grateful for. We may be grateful that we have food in the fridge or power or a roof over our heads. However, how often do you stop and think about everything that you are grateful for about your partner? What is it that happens when you stop to think about what your partner does for you or how your partner is able to help you? Stop and consider this for a few moments and then write it all down into a list that you can share with him or her.

The idea here is that you will be able to tell the other person exactly what you appreciate about them. They will do the same for you, and this means that you will be able to recognize the truth of the matter. You will be able to get those feelings into words in front of you, and your partner will be able to see them written out for him or her as well, and vice versa.

When you can see that your partner truly does appreciate you and respect you, you can start to feel much better and much more confident in the relationship. You will be able to process the ways in which you are able to interact with them—you will see the fact that your relationship is not actually one sided when you realize that there were things that your partner also appreciated about you. This helps build confidence as well—you and your partner will both likely feel much better when you realize how much you mean to each other!

The 7-Step Recovery Map

The 7-Step Recovery Map is your lifeline to relationship recovery. The 7-Step Recovery Map has been developed over the past 25+ years and has emerged out of my (family therapist Abe Kass) direct experience working with couples who have been devastated by every type and permeation of infidelity.

When infidelity was not repeated, couples who have followed this relationship roadmap have always recovered. This is encouraging news and should inspire you to follow each step even when the road seems difficult.

Relationship recovery in some ways parallels medical recovery for a physical ailment. As the doctor prescribes a precise routine of treatment — for example a root canal procedure — the patient is encouraged to conscientiously apply systematically each detail of the treatment plan. The same seriousness is required for successful infidelity recovery. Each detail in The 7-Step Recovery Map is important and should not be discarded because it is either inconvenient, uncomfortable, or seemingly nonsensical. Each of the 7-Steps — without exception — are essential to full relationship recovery.

I know from years of clinical experience that the individual who is in the hot seat — the betrayer — often wants to avoid the difficult parts of recovery. He or she does not want his or her nose rubbed in the shameful mess he or she has created. However, giving in to this instinct will sabotage recovery efforts.

Imagine a fire in your home. Of course, you could just run to the mall and ignore the fire, and at first impulse this may seem to be the desirable solution. But what will happen? Utter devastation. Facing the fire is the only sensible thing to do. Get the fire extinguisher, call the fire department, get everyone out of the house, warn the neighbors, etc. When there is a crisis, we need to face it — not run from it. You and your partner need to face the infidelity crisis if you are to survive. The 7-Step Recovery Map provides the structure and guidance necessary to put out your infidelity ignited relationship fires!

Even if you stay together, although you have not worked through your relationship crisis by facing the infidelity that has occurred, you will never be close again. Your relationship will forever be marred by feelings of mistrust, anger, and worry. You will always be emotionally distant — what a sad way to live!

On the other hand, when you take the time to follow this The 7-Step Recovery Map you will heal completely; or very close to it. When infidelity strikes, and it is not repeated, you can certainly recover... and you should make the efforts to do so. Some couples even emerge out of the infidelity fire healthier and closer than they had ever been in the past.

Certainly, for many reasons, infidelity should not be viewed as a means to improve a relationship. However, for some couples, in spite of the risk to the survival of their relationship and the emotional pain, emerge from the infidelity crisis healthier and happier. Whether it was worth the risk and pain to get to that happy relationship point is for them to decide. My point, their success comes from having followed the 7-Step Recovery Map or an informal, improvised version of it.

This 7-Step Recovery Map is your guide taking you from devastation to the best relationship outcome possible which includes a revitalized relationship imbued with renewed trust, friendship, love, and passion.

I have witnessed hundreds of couples recover from infidelity, and you and your partner can do likewise. If you find recovery too difficult to do on your own (and this is often the case), then hire a skilled, caring, and professional relationship specialist to help you. It will be the best investment you make in your lifetime. When you follow The 7-Step Recovery Map you can go beyond surviving; you can thrive. Get started now...

Sex as a Couple

Some sexual conflicts are major, some minor, but all tap into the heart of a relationship, because even when the hurt seems trivial, when it is sexual, it is not easily forgiven or forgotten.

Are you, as an individual, hoarding a secret sexual hurt? Are you, as a couple, having a problem with sex? Good sex adds to your power as a couple, but bad sex weakens and divides you. Bad sex leaves you with a feeling of loneliness and isolation, and can lead to a depressed state that affects your entire life.

Most Couples Have Trouble with Sex

Although sex may have been what brought you together, it can easily turn into what drives you apart. The main reason for this is not that sex itself is so difficult, but that our culture gives very confusing messages as to what sex is and what it should be.

Since sex is something so closely tied to your feelings and self-esteem, it can be very difficult to talk about. One purpose of this is to give you a place to talk about and deal with the most intimate part of your life.

Most Couples Have Trouble Talking about Sex

If you can't talk about something, it's very unlikely that you can change it. Can you talk with your partner about sex? Not sex in the abstract, but sex as it directly affects your relationship?

When the problem is sexual, how do you break the ice and say what you may have long kept silent? The words you use are important, but even more important is the way you say them. And even more important than that is the way your partner hears them. The most important step in coming together has to do with the attitude you bring to each other.

Breaking the Ice: Your Attitude

If you're having a problem with sex, the first step is to shift from seeing your partner as the problem to seeing your sexual interaction as the problem. You want to attack the problem, not each other. You have nothing to lose by taking the first step and letting go of the struggle against each other.

The following deal with separate, specific aspects of sex, but the focus of this is to help you as a couple to start working on the problem as allies. If you're fighting each other, there's no way to win. The purpose of this is to help you get on the same side of the conflict.

Getting on the Same Side of the Conflict

Sex is viewed very differently by different people. How you were raised, what you were taught, what you've experienced—it all makes a difference. In fact, just being a man or a woman will probably make a difference as to how you view sex. It's as if you see sex through different ends of the telescope, or, to put it another way, you're on different trips, heading for different destinations.

This doesn't have to be the case.

It's quite possible, and very helpful, to lay out certain basic concepts about sex that you can share. Agreeing on these concepts is a way of getting on the same side of the conflict. Then you know at least that you're starting from the same place, talking about the same thing, and heading in the same direction.

What Is Sex?

Contrary to what you may think, this seemingly direct and simple question is a very difficult one to answer. This is one reason why so many couples have difficulty with sex. We each have our own way of conceptualizing it, what we think it should be, and what we want it to be.

Think back to President Bill Clinton's famous response, in the press conference of January 1998, when he stated, "I did not have sexual relations with that woman,"—a statement many would not agree with. (If you are interested, you actually can view Bill Clinton saying this on YouTube).

In looking for a definition as to "What is sex?" we find dictionaries are of little help, since current thinking has so broadened the field that most such definitions are obsolete. The Internet gives more up-to-date information:

So, there we have an answer, but not a simple answer. Just as sexual activities can mean different things to different people, so sexual interaction for couples is an individual matter and can include a variety of sexual activities.

The important thing is that this interaction be successful. That is, that it brings sexual gratification to each partner, increasing their sense of closeness and strengthening their relationship.

The question then becomes, "How is such sexual gratification achieved?"

Sexual gratification is achieved when the need for physical closeness and intimacy is satisfied. It's that simple. Sexual gratification occurs when your need to be intimate and touched by your partner is fulfilled.

For most of us, sex has become entangled with our self-image, feelings of right and wrong, a need to be loved, fears of rejection. Can you put all of that aside for now? Can you see sexual gratification as simply fulfillment of a basic need we all have to be touched, to be intimately close to another, to no longer be physically alone?

Sexual Gratification Is Achieved Primarily Through the Sense of Touch

There is nothing mysterious about sex. It's quite simply the mutual caressing and stimulating of physical receptors in the skin, particularly in the genital area. The experience can reach the level of sexual climax, but does not have to.

If you're willing to let yourself feel and enjoy touch, you can enjoy sex. If you're willing to touch and caress your partner, you can give sexual pleasure. If you are willing to let your partner touch and caress you, you can receive sexual gratification. The pleasure, however, should not just be an occasional or chance occurrence; it needs to be the heart of the experience.

Regardless of the emotional complexities you bring to your relationship, if you're willing, it's within your power to touch and accept the body of your partner. It's within your power, if you're willing, to give them sexual gratification, and it's within your power as well to enjoy the sense of touch and intimacy.

After all, isn't that what you would like: the knowledge that you are wanted and accepted physically? And isn't that what you would like to give your partner: the surety of knowing that they also are wanted and appreciated physically?

When sex is viewed this way (a simple need for physical closeness and intimacy), it's not so very different from any of the other needs (or drives) that you deal with every day of your life.

For example, you've probably been able to come together in regard to eating: when you eat, what you eat, and how you eat. Why not the same with sex? And you've probably been able to come together as to sleeping: when you sleep and how you sleep. Why not the same with sex?

When you can think of sex as a simple physical interchange that brings sensual pleasure to each partner, it'll be easier to deal with. You'll have taken away its power and cut it down to size.

Sex Is Learned

Why do you have to learn how to have sex? The reason is that, although you may be born with the drive that leads to having sex, you are not born knowing how to have sex. You are not born knowing how to touch your partner.

Each person is different; each person's response to touch is different. When you have sex with a partner, you have to learn how to fulfill their sensual need to be touched. You need to learn how to touch them.

There is one condition, however, that must be fulfilled before you can enjoy touch. That is: you have to feel safe. You have to be in a safe "holding environment," which means you know you are with someone who cares about you, someone who is accepting of you, someone who would never hurt or ridicule you.

Your caring about each other is more important than sex. If it were primarily sex you were interested in, you could find that elsewhere. What you really want is to have good sex with this partner because you love and want to please them.

The Primary Goal of Sex Is Pleasure

Sex can have many goals: to please your partner, to get pregnant, to release sexual tension, to affirm the fact that you're desirable, etc. All of these may be important, but to make the sexual act itself successful, one goal needs to be primary: pleasure.

When you agree to make pleasure the primary goal, you agree also to let go of all other goals, both for yourself and for your partner. For example, if pleasure is the primary goal, it really doesn't matter whether you reach orgasm. It doesn't matter whether you are old or young. It doesn't matter whether you are rich or poor. It doesn't matter whether you are fat or thin. The only requirement for each of you is that you try to give your partner sensual pleasure, and that you find such pleasure for yourself as well.

Do you agree (more or less) with the above comments? Can you add some of your own? If so, you are ready for the workshop, which will guide you in breaking the ice and talking about sex. Good luck!

Conclusion

When two people meet in a relationship with an element of passion that sustains them and their union ends in marriage, they may not be aware of what is to follow. Sometimes they may have difficulty keeping everything together or reconciling. Love is messy and infidelity is even more disorderly. To ensure normality again, it is necessary to have something to hold onto. Some infidelities resolve quickly, but some may have difficulty ending. This reluctance must be worked out. People who want to rebuild the relationship after the unfaithfulness are on a hard journey. At the time of being destroyed, you don't trust what the unfaithful says. You lose confidence in others and in yourself. It is a loss of a partner and a loss of self. Try to find a purpose and never lose hope. If the person left you without giving you the answers you deserved, embrace it. Feel hurt and move on. A healthy and safe future awaits you.

Having a relationship without criticism, without resentment, without cheating is just a place where you two will be happy to be together and support each other. Each of us should try to reach that place in our relationships where there is complete honesty and space to breathe. If you feel that being honest is difficult or unworkable for you, there are a few things you can do to significantly increase the amount of honesty and enjoy all the good things in your relationship. The first is to be honest with yourself and to yourself. The relationship you have with others is a reflection of yours with yourself. If you want something in life and you think you can't tell your spouse, maybe because they may not approve, then move that thought away; just ask yourself what you really want here. Imagine it theoretically, and it becomes really clear. So, imagine the worst thing that can happen if you tell your partner what you're hiding. You may think they will get angry. Maybe they will or not. But if they get angry, they will have to deal with it and the chances are they will get over it. Getting angry is something that can be addressed. So, you have to understand what the best thing is that could happen. You can actually get what you want and share happiness with your partner. An example of this is when a husband in therapy revealed that he wanted to go to a nudist beach and go scuba diving and sunbathing. He felt embarrassed to say it out loud because he feared his wife would judge him. So, it is really necessary to provide total honesty. The step is to create an environment of trust. You decide to never make your spouse feel bad about what they say or do. Don't judge them for their thoughts and feelings. Allow them to make mistakes. The last step is to guarantee total honesty from this point onwards.

I wish you the best of luck, and I hope this has helped your soul to heal and your relationship to become stronger.

Thank you for purchasing this, and I hope that reading it was an interesting and educational experience. I put all my efforts, enthusiasm and heart into every sentence I wrote. The main objective of this is to help, with my experience, my readers to understand and overcome betrayal, which is a profound and devastating malaise. If you liked it, and above all, it influenced your life and helped you along the way, I ask you for five minutes of your time to write down what you think by leaving, because it would help other people improve their lives. The opinions of my readers are ones I always treasure for my work, and it would help me improve my way of communicating and give me new ideas to develop.